ADB INTERNATIONAL INVESTMENT AGREEMENT TOOL KIT

A COMPARATIVE APPROACH

MAY 2021

ADB

ASIAN DEVELOPMENT BANK

Contents

Tables and Figures

Tables

Figures

Foreword

International investment agreements safeguard mutual economic interests of investors and host economies and, as such, are an important tool for shaping foreign direct investment (FDI) policy. Such agreements govern issues including the scope of investment, treatment of foreign investors, and dispute settlement and compensation mechanisms. For investors, they grant international legal protection from adverse actions by governments. For host states, these agreements can signal a stable and predictable environment for investment and promote governance standards.

In recent years, however, as the number of investor-state disputes has increased, concerns have arisen that international investment agreements may impose costs on states and not always fully deliver on their objectives. Meanwhile, Asia's investment treaty regime has also gained prominence in the wake of the coronavirus disease (COVID-19). The pandemic has forced many governments in the region to take extraordinary measures on foreign investment to balance public health and economic interests. Should the pandemic trigger investor-state disputes in the region, we should expect governments and investors to resort to existing agreements. Investment agreements will also be instrumental in reinvigorating FDI for the post-pandemic economic recovery.

This report provides a new framework for analyzing the network of international investment regimes in Asia and the Pacific. With this aim, a comprehensive database of investment agreements—including bilateral investment treaties and investment chapters in free trade agreements—has been developed to provide a more granular codification of investment provisions in the region.

The ADB International Investment Agreement Tool Kit details investment provisions and qualitatively assesses their possible implications for FDI flows, with numerous examples from the region. The report expands knowledge with novel information on investment provisions, such as public interest obligations and transparency in investor-state arbitration. It also proposes new approaches to analyze investment regimes, introducing indicators in relevant treaty areas such as investment liberalization, anti-discrimination, regulatory constraint, and investor-state dispute settlement quality.

The region's network of investment agreements draws attention in the wake of COVID-19 as economic crises often increase tensions and interruptions in global businesses, triggering an upsurge of investor–state disputes. The design and negotiation of investment agreements is often highly complex. But this report employs new approaches to compare their design and structure and to assess the efficiency of provisions and their possible economic impact. Investment provisions can be better designed and negotiated to accommodate different investment conditions and requirements between home and host economies and, if properly designed, prevent investor-state disputes in the aftermath of COVID-19 and attract more and better quality FDI into the region. Modernizing investment provisions in current and future investment agreements is essential to this end and ADB will continue to support such efforts to encourage a better investment climate in the region.

Yasuyuki Sawada
Chief Economist and Director General
Economic Research and Regional Cooperation Department
Asian Development Bank

Acknowledgments

This publication was prepared by the Regional Cooperation and Integration Division (ERCI) of the Economic Research and Regional Cooperation Department (ERCD) of the Asian Development Bank (ADB), with support from Technical Assistance 9210: Enhancing Research Alliance and South–South Development Policy Cooperation Between Asia and the Pacific and Latin America.

Under the guidance of Cyn-Young Park, director of ERCI, the preparation of this report was led by Rolando Avendano (economist, ERCI, ERCD) and Fahad Khan (economist, Economic Analysis and Operational Support Division (EREA)/ERCD), with the support of Paulo Rodelio Halili (senior economics officer, ADB).

The report is based on the research led by Professor Julien Chaisse (City University of Hong Kong), with contributions from Junkyu Lee, chief of Finance Sector Group of the Sustainable Development and Climate Change Department; Fahad Khan, economist, EREA/ERCD; Rolando Avendano, economist, ERCI/ERCD; Mikko Marl Diaz and Lovely Ann Tolin.

The report team is grateful for the helpful feedback provided by participants at the ADB workshops on *Foreign Direct Investment in the time of COVID-19: Policy Options for Asia* (July 2020) and *Bilateral Investment Agreements and Asia's FDI* (September 2020). Authors are especially grateful to Maria Borga, Balance of Payments division, IMF; Rodolphe Desbordes, Professor of Economics, SKEMA Business School; Yothin Jinjarak, senior economist ERMR/ERCD; Jong Woo Kang, principal economist ERCI/ERCD; and Christina Pak, principal counsel, Office of the General Counsel. Contributions from Mara Claire Tayag (senior economics officer, ADB) and Clemence Fatima Cruz are also acknowledged.

Rolando Avendano and Paulo Rodelio Halili coordinated the production of this report, with administrative support from Marilyn Aure Parra (senior operations assistant, ADB).

James Unwin edited the report. Michael Cortes created the cover design and implemented the typesetting and layout. Jess Macasaet proofread the report, while Corazon Desuasido handled the page proof checking. Support for printing and publishing was provided by the Printing Services Unit of ADB's Office of Administrative Services and by the Publishing team of the Department of Communications.

Abbreviations

ADB	Asian Development Bank
ASEAN	Association of Southeast Asian Nations
BIT	bilateral investment treaty
BRICS	Brazil, Russia, India, China, and South Africa
CPTPP	Comprehensive and Progressive Trans-Pacific Partnership
EPA	economic partnership agreement
ERCD	Economic Research and Regional Cooperation Department
EU	European Union
FCN	Friendship, Commerce and Navigation
FDI	foreign direct investment
FET	fair and equitable treatment
FTA	free trade agreement
GATT	General Agreement on Tariffs and Trade
HK	Hong Kong, China
ICSID	International Centre for Settlement of Investment Disputes
IIA	international investment agreement
IISD	International Institute for Sustainable Investment
ISD	investor state dispute
ISDM	investor–state dispute mechanisms
ISDS	investor-state dispute settlement
MFN	most favored nation
NAFTA	North American Free Trade Agreement
NT	national treatment
OECD	Organisation for Economic Co-operation and Development
PCA	Permanent Court of Arbitration
PR	performance requirements
PRC	People's Republic of China
PTA	preferential trade agreement
SCC	Stockholm Chamber of Commerce
TRIMs	trade-related investment measures
UK	United Kingdom
UNCITRAL	United Nations Commission on International Trade Law
UNCTAD	United Nations Conference on Trade and Development
US	United States
WTO	World Trade Organization

Executive Summary

International investment agreements (IIAs) are an important policy tool to attract foreign direct investment (FDI). They are designed to address issues relevant to cross-border investments, typically aimed at safeguarding the economic interests of both the recipient economies and international investors, while promoting open and rule-based international investment. However, design and negotiation of IIAs form a complex, technical, and evolving subject. Usually, they cover a broad set of issues, with provisions on the standards of protection and treatment of foreign investments, including fair and equitable treatment, investor protection and security, national treatment, and most favored nation treatment. With the rapid expansion of IIAs, their types and contents vary considerably and are becoming increasingly complex and often difficult to understand. In this respect, better data need to be developed to cover these types and contents more comprehensively and effectively by codifying the full range of IIAs. This will help researchers and policymakers analyze and compare the design, structure, and economic impact of IIAs. ADB's Regional Cooperation and Integration Division of the Economic Research and Regional Cooperation Department (ERCD) led a research project to create a comprehensive database of IIAs, including both bilateral investment treaties (BITs) and investment chapters of free trade agreements (FTAs). The project aimed to create a granular codification of 15 investment provisions through a detailed textual analysis of all Asian IIAs currently signed and enforced. The database captures the most important dimensions in Asia's IIAs and will be adapted into a web-based tool disseminated by the Asian Development Bank. The provisions codified by the index are as follows: (i) Definition of Investment, (ii) Admission versus Establishment, (iii) National Treatment, (iv) Most Favored Nation Treatment, (v) Fair and Equitable Treatment, (vi) Direct and Indirect Expropriation, (vii) Free Transfer of Investment-Related Funds, (viii) Noneconomic Standards, (ix) Investor-State Dispute Mechanism, (x) Umbrella Clause, (xi) Temporal Scope of Application, (xii) Performance Requirements (xiii) Transparency Mechanisms, (xiv) Public Interest Obligations, and (xv) Exception Clause.

1. Introduction

Foreign investment is an important pillar for the development of Asian economies. It brings benefits through the creation of new jobs, expanded opportunities among domestic enterprises, infrastructure development, and technology transfer. With a strategy to attract and preserve foreign investment, a country can cooperate with others through established mechanisms called investment treaties, which are often referred to as international investment agreements (IIAs). In 2016, G20 trade ministers reinforced their determination to "promote inclusive, robust and sustainable trade and investment growth" and agreed on the G20 Guiding Principles for Global Investment Policymaking.[1] As these principles have been endorsed, the Asia and Pacific region is adapting its investment frameworks to follow through on this important stepping stone to greater investment policy coherence. This study aims to contribute to this effort.

An investment treaty is a legal instrument to govern the particular circumstances of investment, such as its scope, treatments received by foreign investors, and dispute settlement and compensation mechanisms.[2] The main purpose of IIAs is to create "a stable and predictable environment for investment" by providing protection to foreign investors and safeguarding the interests of the host economies in line with their development objectives. Meanwhile, as signatories, states show not only that the investment environment is good but also that guarantees for foreign investors exist. The number of IIAs has increased significantly since the first was concluded in 1959. As of December 2020, more than 3,000 IIAs have been signed by more than 170 countries.[3] This number includes bilateral investment treaties (BITs) and investment chapters in preferential trade agreements (PTAs).

The negotiations for the Comprehensive and Progressive Trans-Pacific Partnership (CPTPP) or the Transatlantic Trade and Investment Partnership (TTIP), the recent conclusion of the Regional Comprehensive Economic Partnership (RCEP) in November 2020, and other investment treaties such as BITs that the People's Republic of China (PRC) has been negotiating with the United States and the European Union (EU), show there is still relatively scarce knowledge among lawyers and policymakers about the potential impact of IIAs on foreign direct investment (FDI).[4]

---

[1] Nine nonbinding Guiding Principles guide investment policy making with a view to fostering an open, transparent, and conducive global policy environment for investment, promoting coherence in national and international investment policies, and promoting inclusive economic growth and sustainable development. See UNCTAD. 2016. UNCTAD Facilitates G20 Consensus on Guiding Principles for Global Investment Policymaking. *UNCTAD News Report.* 11 July.

[2] Wang, G. 2010. International Investment Law: An Appraisal from the Perspective of the New Haven School of International Law. *Asia Pacific Law Review.* 18 (1). pp. 19-44.

[3] UNCTAD. 2020. International Investment Agreements Navigator. 8 December. https://investmentpolicy.unctad.org/international-investment-agreements.

[4] For example, see Wei, Y. 2018. Challenges, Issues in China-EU Investment Agreement and the Implication on China's Domestic Reform. *Asia Pacific Law Review.* 26 (2). pp. 170-202.

New policy challenges are also appearing in the region.[5] The COVID-19 pandemic has forced many governments to respond with extraordinary stringent measures to balance public health and economic interests. Governments have introduced approaches to handle the pandemic by imposing various travel restrictions, hard border closures, import-export restrictions, or the nationalization of private businesses. These measures may violate foreign investment protections accorded to investors under IIAs.[6] Indeed IIAs offer a broad spectrum of legal protection to foreign investors that can strengthen their rights under any contract that regulates the investment.

The conclusion of many BITs and FTAs and the fast-evolving policy context for foreign investment call for a finer understanding of what governments can do in terms of IIAs' negotiation and implementation to increase the benefits of FDI. Empirical approaches to assessing this are not always conclusive.[7] Several reasons explain the divergence of expert views:

- First, provisions in BITs and FTAs are in general tailor-made to serve the specific interests of contracting parties. All stakeholders will agree that while IIAs by and large have similar structures, the devil is in the details: provisions do not only differ but greatly vary, disrupting the whole international investment regime with a complexity that few other international regimes know. Thus, it is insufficient to determine the impact of BITs and FTAs only as separate variables in economic models. Detailed qualitative analysis of BIT and FTA provisions is necessary to examine their real impact on FDI.

- Second, because BITs and FTAs include various provisions, it is critical to examine the interrelationships among various provisions and agreements in assessing their impact. Investment provisions in BITs and FTAs are interrelated and their impacts on FDI are intertwined. In the case of FTAs, besides the investment chapter, other chapters may also affect FDI policy. Given the increasing importance of global value chains in investment decisions, trade liberalization (tariff) and trade facilitation chapters in an FTA may have an impact on FDI. Various types of harmonization are also likely to impact FDI because they reduce the cost of doing business, an important factor in investment decisions. An FTA's services chapter (Mode 3) could also overlap with investment chapters. Furthermore, one country may sign various types of IIAs with different partners that may have provisions for most favored nation (MFN) status and two countries may sign a multiple number of IIAs that interact with each other (e.g., both BIT and FTA).

- Third, whether provisions of BITs and FTAs become effective in attracting FDI also depends on external conditions such as the quality of governance of host countries. While it is not easy to generalize that BITs and FTAs are complements or substitutes for domestic governance, the way in which the two are interrelated is complex. For example, the investor-state dispute (ISD) clause may be a substitute for a domestic juridical system (when domestic juridical system does not work well, ISD is usually effective), while the liberalization clause may complement

5   Saurav, A., P. Kusek, R. Kuo, and B. Viney. 2020. The Impact of COVID-19 on Foreign investors: Evidence from the Second Round of a Global Pulse Survey. *World Bank Blogs.* 6 October. https://blogs.worldbank.org/psd/impactcovid-19-foreign-investors-evidence-second-round-global-pulse-survey.

6   For example, see Prabhash R. and P. Anand. 2020. COVID-19, India, and Investor-State Dispute Settlement (ISDS): Will India be Able to Defend its Public Health Measures? *Asia Pacific Law Review.* 28 (1). pp. 225-47. DOI:10.1080/1019 2557.2020.1812255. See also Bernasconi-Osterwalder, N., S. Brewin, N. Maina. 2020. Protecting Against Investor–State Claims Amidst COVID-19: A Call to Action for Governments. International Institute for Sustainable Investment (IISD) Commentary. April. https://www.iisd.org/system/files/publications/investor-state-claims-covid-19.pdf.

7   Bellak (2015) explains that "In general, empirical results suffer from the fact that the research process is prone to biases. (Stanley and Jarell 1989). Therefore, particular emphasis will be put on correcting the results for publication bias. This is necessary, as publication selection leads to the main—if not the only—bias of empirical results and thus may seriously distort the evidence and following from it, would lead to misleading policy conclusions. In this endeavor, the technique of meta-analysis will be used to uncover the genuine economic effect of BITs on the basis of existing evidence."

the domestic system (when institutional quality is good, the liberalization clause has an impact on FDI). Hence, provision-level analysis is necessary for examining the importance of external conditions.

A new index, the ADB IIA Tool Kit, has been developed to understand these differences.[8] The common element to questions about IIA provisions relates to the contents and substance of the agreements. ADB's IIA Tool Kit aims to guide economists and governments to develop a view about which common types of IIA provision could be adopted in regional or multilateral agreements at lower cost. The tool kit should also allow legal scholars to progress from particular aspects of an IIA toward a more universal and applied view of this part of international investment law. It also aims to inform firms to directly compare IIAs across a large number of countries, where affiliates may be located.

Several initiatives exist today to improve our understanding of IIAs, including comprehensive initiatives by the United Nations Conference on Trade and Development (UNCTAD) or the Organisation for Economic Co-operation and Development.[9] A key difference with the ADB Tool Kit is that differences between IIAs are established not only by mapping whether a certain provision has been included, but by evaluating whether the provision grants extensive or circumscribed rights to the investor. The complexity of the international investment regime is dealt with by deconstructing each treaty and providing a relative assessment on the role of each provision.

The ADB IIA Tool Kit allows users to gather data for a large number of IIAs at essentially two levels: **provision** and **agreement**.

- First, the *provision-level indicators* allow a precise and detailed analysis of specific provisions. For instance, many definitions of the concept of investment can be extracted and compared across specific countries, regions or over time in order to identify trends and changing patterns. The provision-level also allows attention to be brought to the specific meaning and likely impact of each provision by grouping them in indicators which shed light on key specificities of IIAs. For instance, instead of comparing the definitions of national treatment, a combined indicator on liberalization or anti-discrimination of a treaty can be preferred.

- Second, the Tool Kit allows researchers to reanalyze a considerable volume of IIAs by comparing indicators at the *agreement level*. This approach allows a specific score to be identified for each investment treaty and comparison with other agreements across different dimensions (country, region, level of economic development, year, and so on). As examples, an IIA Quality Indicator and an indicator of heterogeneity are presented in this manual. In addition, the concept of *modulation of coefficients* is introduced as another refinement to allow full flexibility in analyses.

The ADB IIA Tool Kit is distinctively flexible and adaptable. If the IIA Quality Indicator relies on the score of 15 key provisions, a concern may be that the same importance is given to all provisions. Users could suggest, for example, that the MFN provision is far more important than a provision on the duration of the treaty. Indeed, the MFN clause can have a considerable impact on investment decisions or arbitration results when it is extensively drafted and included in a treaty concluded by a country that has a dense network of IIAs. The likely effect of a MFN clause can be assumed to be greater than, say, a provision on the duration. The ADB IIA Tool Kit and associated indicators

---

[8]   Visit https://aric.adb.org/database/iias for the ADB IIA Tool Kit companion database.

[9]   See UNCTAD http://investmentpolicyhub.unctad.org/IIA and https://www.oecd.org/investment/ .

account for this by giving the two values different weights, while the Tool Kit allows researchers to adjust the relative weight for each score or agreement-level indicator.

The ADB IIA Tool Kit considers the complexity of the international investment regime and provides public access to reliable data that should inform those involved in the design and implementation of treaties, serving to enrich debate and understanding about international investment policy.

The ADB IIA Tool Kit aims to provide comparable information on the structure of investment treaties and the balance of provisions to ensure interests of both states and investors are safeguarded. The Tool Kit provides a possible assessment of how provisions may be more or less favorable to FDI environment. This information does not aim at proposing a normative approach to treaty design or optimal treaty structures. While certain provisions may not be relevant from an investor perspective, for example, they could be essential for some states to attain certain development objectives.

In this sense, the approach in the codification of provisions does not suggest in any way that policy makers should refrain from regulating relevant aspects of IIAs. The IIA Tool Kit and database is aimed for technical guidance and users can decide how to employ the information based on their policy objectives. For further policy considerations, important efforts to reform the investment treaty agenda are being discussed (OECD 2019, UNCTAD 2020, Berger and Sauvant 2021) to provide a more balanced approach that takes into consideration investment protection while ensuring host states' development objectives.

This manual builds upon earlier work of Chaisse and Bellak (2015) and provides a comprehensive analysis of investment treaties and arbitration design and explains the rationale in creating the Tool Kit. Section 2 begins by explaining the practical importance of investment treaties. Section 3 expands the analysis by reviewing each of the 15 key provisions coded in the Tool Kit. Section 4 concludes and draws policy recommendations.

2. Relevance of Investment Treaties to Asia and the Pacific: Understanding the Trends

Foreign investment is an important driver in shaping the international economic landscape (Elkins, Guzman, and Simmons 2006). Asia is now the global hub for attracting foreign investment.[10] Global FDI grew by 3.0% in 2019, after declining in 2018. Asia's inward foreign investment accounted for nearly 33.2% of the global total, estimated at $1.5 trillion in 2019, confirming Asia's status as the largest recipient region the world (Asian Development Bank 2021). Additionally, Asian economies have made important steps toward becoming major players in the global investment scene (Bath and Nottage 2019). Some of the largest investors today are the PRC; Hong Kong, China; Japan; and Singapore.

Asian economies have taken several measures to attract and retain foreign investment as they have gained prominence. The establishment of the Asian Infrastructure Investment Bank,[11] passing of new investment laws, and gradual removal of FDI restrictions in some, if not all, sensitive sectors are a few examples.[12] Trade and investment links within Asia have also expanded rapidly, with Asia second only to Europe in intraregional trade volumes.

In general, FDI regulatory restrictiveness across the world has increased in the past 2 decades, with Asian countries implementing, and subsequently easing, strict investment measures. The OECD FDI Restrictiveness Index provides an overview on the regulatory restrictiveness of a country, including foreign equity limitations, discriminatory screening or approval mechanisms, foreign employment restrictions in key positions, and other restrictions on operations. Under this measure, FDI restrictiveness has been generally higher in Asia than in other regions and peaked in 2014, with regulatory restrictions easing since. To some extent, FDI to Asia has climbed at the same time that regulatory restrictions have eased.

Asian states have also concluded a considerable number of IIAs (Bath and Nottage 2011). Indeed, more than a third of the nearly 3,000 investment treaties currently in existence involve Asian signatories. The PRC has concluded the most investment treaties, followed by the Republic of Korea and India (Chaisse 2015a).

---

[10] For the present purposes, "Asia" includes those countries grouped as Eastern Asia, Southern Asia, and South-Eastern Asia, as defined by the United Nations Conference on Trade and Development (UNCTAD).

[11] See Asian Infrastructure Investment Bank. 2015. *Articles of Agreement.* 22 May. http://www.aiib.org/html/aboutus/ Basic_Documents/; ASEAN Secretariat. 2011. *ASEAN Master Plan on ASEAN Connectivity.* January. http://www.asean. org/resources/publications/asean-publications/item/master-plan-on-asean-connectivity-2; National Development and Reform Commission, Ministry of Foreign Affairs, and Ministry of Commerce of People's Republic of China. 2015. *Vision and Actions on Jointly Building Silk Road Economic Belt and 21st-Century Maritime Silk Road.* 28 March. http://en.ndrc.gov. cn/newsrelease/201503/t20150330_669367.html; and Ministry of Foreign Affairs of Republic of Korea. 2015. EurAsia Initiative. 2 August. http://www.mofa.go.kr/ENG/image/common/title/res/0707_eurasia_bro.pdf.

[12] UNCTAD. 2016. Latest issue of UNCTAD Investment Policy Monitor. http://unctad.org/en/pages/newsdetails.aspx?Origi nalVersionID=1218&Sitemap_x0020_Taxonomy=UNCTAD%20Home;#6;#Investment and Enterprise.

Along with increasing foreign investment, another significant development is the growth of disputes between foreign investors and host states (Kaushal 2009; Jandhyala, Henisz, and Mansfield 2011; Reinisch, 2013; Nottage 2016). These disputes, commonly resolved by resorting to arbitration under the investor–state dispute settlement (ISDS) process, have climbed in number over the past decade.[13] Asia and the Pacific itself has witnessed a significant rise in claims. At least 110 investment disputes involving 25 states in the region have been filed since 1987. Overall, about 15% of all investment disputes involve Asian states.

While arbitration remains the preferred dispute resolution mechanism for resolving investor–state disputes, a number of states have proposed viable alternatives (Vandevelde 2005; Bernasconi-Osterwalder and Rosert 2014).[14] Several are redefining the current ISDS framework and its relationship to democratic decision-making (Haftel and Thompson 2013). In the Asian context, for instance, the EU-Viet Nam IIA contemplates the creation of an "investment court" to resolve disputes between investors and states. Other states have chosen to significantly reduce the scope of investor–state disputes, while still others now require such disputes to be first submitted for resolution in their own domestic courts.[15] It is timely to review the current trends and recent developments in the ISDS framework, and to consider their effects on both Asian states and Asian investors.

---

[13] Reinisch, A. 2013. The Scope of Investor-State Dispute Settlement in International Investment Agreements. *Asia Pacific Law Review.* 21 (1): pp. 3-26. https://doi.org/10.1080/10192557.2013.11788264.

[14] Foreign investors are increasingly resorting to the mechanism of international arbitration for resolving their disputes with the government of a host country.

[15] 2015 Indian Model Bilateral Investment Treaty.

3. Reviewing the 15 IIAS Key Provisions

The ADB IIA Tool Kit is structured around these main concepts:

- International investment agreements (IIAs) are structured into provisions, which can take the form of a full paragraph, single sentence, or even part of a sentence.

- The term "article" in law is a separate and distinct part of a written instrument, such as a contract, statute, or a treaty such as IIA.

- The term "provision" is often used as an alternative to "article" when referring to the content of particular articles (series of "articles" or "provisions" lay out the obligations of those states choosing to be bound by it and procedural matters involving the treaty).

- Regarding terminated IIAs, if the terminated IIA is replaced by a new IIA, the new one is coded in the ADB IIA Tool Kit. This concerns approximatively 200 IIAs in the database. Otherwise the terminated IIA is coded.

- Only IIAs in English-language versions are coded in the ADB Tool Kit. IIAs in other languages are not coded.

3.1 Definition of Investment

Every IIA contains the definition of both investors and investment and scope of application, which are stated in the first article. Conclusions about the definition and scope of application in IIAs would identify their coverage (Knorich and Berger 2014). In the beginning of IIAs' formulation, comprehensive definitions of investment and investors did not exist, but these are now defined in a wider scope (Subedi 2012).

For instance, the definition of investment includes FDI, portfolio investment, and intellectual property rights (Subedi 2012). It is as stated in the US BIT Model 2004, which has an extensive definition of investment as referring to "every asset that an investor owns to control, directly or indirectly, that has the characteristics of an investment, including such characteristics as the commitment of capital or other resources, the expectation of gain of profit, or the assumption of risk."[16]

Most IIAs have traditionally been aimed at investment protection and define "investment" in an extensive and open-ended manner, covering not only capital that has crossed borders, but also, practically all other kinds of assets of an investor in the territory of the host country.

---

[16] United States BIT Model 2004, Article 1.

Among IIAs, several kinds of definitions can be distinguished:

1. Asset-based: Defining asset classes. A definition that—with several variations—continues to be the most common approach.
2. Circular or tautological: An approach that focuses on the features of an investment rather than conceptualizing it. Its use has been reduced in recent years.
3. Closed-list: a list of defined investment.
4. Techniques excluding certain assets and transactions from the definition.

In what follows, a hypothesis related to each provision will be presented as a series of examples in existent treaties to illustrate the use of the index.

Hypothesis

An extensive definition of investment provides more rights to investors.
When investment definition is circumscribed, it is a weak incentive to invest (less investments will be covered and protected), and therefore, the risk is higher for the investor.

Examples

See below: Examples 1 and 2 represent the extensive definition.
See below: Examples 3 and 4 represent the circumscribed definition.

How to use the index:

We consider that techniques 1 and 2 provide extensive definition of investment, while techniques 3 and 4 tend to circumscribe the definition of investment and hence automatically reduce the scope of application of the IIA.

Ratings. Circumscribed = 1. Extensive = 2.

Examples: Extensive Definition

Technique 1

- Most BITs of the last 10 years have continued to adopt an extensive "asset-based" definition of "investment," which goes beyond covering FDI only.

- The definition covers "every kind of asset" or "any kind of asset + a list of examples."

- Such lists usually include five categories of assets (as in the Hong Kong, China–Austria BIT):
  a. Movable and immovable property and any related property rights such as mortgages, liens or pledges.
  b. Various types of interests in companies, such as shares, stock, bonds, debentures or any other form of participation in a company, business enterprise or joint venture.

c.   Claims to money and claims under a contract having a financial value and loans directly related to a specific investment.

d.   Intellectual property rights.

e.   Business concessions—rights conferred by law or under contracts.

- Example: **Pakistan–Bahrain BIT (2014)**: Article 1 states:
"The term 'investment' shall comprise every kind of asset invested by the Government or by a natural or juridical person of one Contracting State in the territory of the other Contracting State in accordance with the laws, regulations and administrative practices of that State. Without restricting the generality of the foregoing, the term 'investment' shall include: (a) …"

- Some BITs only refer to "all direct investment" (as in the Hungary–Bulgaria BIT), which states: "1. The term 'investment' shall mean every kind of asset … [T]hese assets shall refer to all direct investment made in accordance with the laws and regulations in the territory of the Contracting Party…"

Technique 2

The definition of "investment" can be flexible enough to apply to new types of investment that *might* emerge in the future. In this respect:

- Some countries have responded to this need by introducing a tautological (or circular) definition of "investment."

- Numerous BITs concluded by the United States illustrate this approach, such as the BIT with Bahrain (1999). It defines an investment as "every kind of *investment*" and not only "every kind of *asset.*"

- This tautological approach is virtually limited to US BITs.

Examples: Circumscribed Definition

Technique 3
- Third approach that has emerged to avoid an excessively extensive definition of "investment" is what is called a "closed-list" definition.
   a.   It consists of an ample, but finite, *list of tangible and intangible assets.*
   b.   Originally envisaged as an "enterprise-based" definition used in the context of US–Canada FTA, this approach evolved toward the definition used in Article 1139 of the North American Free Trade Agreement (NAFTA).

- It has been incorporated into the 2004 Canadian BIT model.

Technique 4
- It excludes certain sectors from the definition of investment.

- Techniques 3 and 4 can be combined as in NAFTA: a positive definition of investment + exclusion.

In **NAFTA**,

Investment means
(a) an enterprise;
(b) an equity security of an enterprise;
(c) a debt security of an enterprise:
- where the enterprise is an affiliate of the investor, or
- where the original maturity of the debt security is at least 3 years,
- yet this excludes debt securities of state enterprises, regardless of original maturity.

Investment does not mean
(a) claims to money that arise solely from
- commercial contracts for the sale of goods or services by a national or enterprise in the territory of a Party to an enterprise in the territory of another Party, or
- the extension of credit in connection with a commercial transaction, such as trade financing, other than a loan covered by subparagraph (d); or
(b) any other claims to money,
- that do not involve the kinds of interests set out in subparagraphs (a) through (h);

In the **Canada–PRC BIT (2012)**, Article 1 combines Techniques 3 and 4, and for the purpose of this agreement,

Investment means
(a) an enterprise;
(b) shares, stocks, and other forms of equity participation in an enterprise;
(c) bonds, debentures, and other debt instruments of an enterprise;
(d) a loan to an enterprise
- where the enterprise is an affiliate of the investor, or
- where the original maturity of the loan is at least 3 years;
(e) notwithstanding points (c) and (d) above, a loan to or debt security issued by a financial institution is an investment only where the loan or debt security is treated as regulatory capital by the Contracting Party in whose territory the financial institution is located;
(f) an interest in an enterprise that entitles the owner to share in the income or profits of the enterprise;
(g) an interest in an enterprise that entitles the owner to share in the assets of that enterprise on dissolution;
(h) interests arising from the commitment of capital or other resources in the territory of a Contracting Party to economic activity in such territory, such as under
- contracts involving the presence of an investor's property in the territory of the Contracting Party, including turnkey or construction contracts, or concessions to search for and extract oil and other natural resources, or
- contracts where remuneration depends substantially on the production, revenue or profits of an enterprise;
(i) intellectual property rights; and
(j) any other tangible or intangible, movable or immovable, property and related property rights acquired or used for business purposes.

continued on the next page

Continued

Investment does not mean

(a) claims to money that arise solely from
- commercial contracts for the sale of goods or services, or
- the extension of credit in connection with a commercial transaction, such as trade financing, other than a loan covered by subparagraph (d); or

(b) any other claims to money, that do not involve the kinds of interests set out in points (a) to (j).

3.2 Admission versus Establishment

According to international law, every state has rights to regulate the admission of foreigners because its rights to national sovereignty also apply to the investment sector (Sacerdoti 2000). Hence, host states have an absolute right in selecting foreign investment in their territories. However, if the capital-importing countries accept the entry of foreign investors into their territory, they must protect them in the form of a standard of treatment under international law (Sacerdoti 2000). There are two models of investment admission under the IIAs. The first is the "right of establishment" model or "pre-establishment right," which automatically provides national treatment (NT) and most favored nation (MFN) treatment to foreign investors not only in entry stage but also when the investment starts operating in capital-importing countries (Chaisse 2015a). The purpose of applying this model is to liberalize investment flows (Chaisse 2015a).

This model is applied by the United States, Canada, Japan, and several preferential trade agreements with investment chapters (Newcombie and Paradell 2009). One of the examples of article of pre-establishment right model states:

Each Party undertakes to provide and maintain a favorable environment for investments in this territory by nationals and companies of the other Party and shall, in applying its laws, regulations, administrative practices and procedures, permit such investments to be established and acquired on terms and conditions that accord treatment no less than that accorded in like situations to investments of nationals or companies of any third country, whichever is more favorable.[17]

Meanwhile, another model is the "admission clause," which stipulates that foreign investment entering into a host state must be in accordance with the national law of host countries (Chaisse 2015a). Most countries, including in Europe, Asia, and Africa, apply this model in their BITs (Dolzer and Schreuer 2012). The typical clause in this model can be found in the Germany Model Treaty of 2005, which states "Each Contracting State shall in its territory promote as far as possible investments by investors of [the] other Contracting State and admit such investments in accordance with its legislation" (Dolzer and Schreuer 2012). Generally, the admission clause model includes a particular requirement for foreign investors to get writing approval from the host country's

---

[17] *Treaty between the United States of America and the Arab Republic of Egypt Concerning the Reciprocal Encouragement and Protection of Investment*, signed 11 March 1986 (entered into force 27 June 1992), Article II.1.

agency in order to ensure that foreign investments conform to the procedures of national law (Chaisse 2015a).

A further example is provided by all of Indonesia's existing BITs, which adopt the admission clause model because foreign investment must be in accordance with Indonesian law and regulations. This is proven by the typical admission provisions in the BITs concluded by Indonesia since it signed its first BIT in 1960. Under the BIT between Indonesia and Denmark, as the first Indonesia's BIT concluded in 1968,[18] the provision regarding admission of foreign investment stated:

> The protection accorded to investors by the provisions of this Agreement shall apply in the territory of the Republic of Indonesia only to investments which have been approved by the Indonesian Government in accordance with the foreign investment legislation currently in force (Law No. 1 of the year 1967).[19]

Also, in Indonesia's BIT with Finland, the admission provision stipulated under Article II (1) stated that "Each Contracting Party shall in its territory admit investments by investors of the other Contracting Party in accordance with its laws and regulations and encourage such investments."[20] Based on the explanation above, Indonesia has been applying admission clause model in the post-establishment phase of foreign investment.

By applying this model, host countries in the process of establishing foreign investment need a selection method consistent with their domestic laws (Chaisse 2015a). In this regard, foreigner investors must fulfill several requirements, such as applying for a certificate of investment, conforming to the lists of investment, and maximum equity conditions (Knorich and Berger 2014; Chaisse 2015a, 2015b). These requirements are also applied to the foreign investment in Indonesia. According to Law No. 25/2007, foreign investors should meet the requirements, for instance, establishing a limited liability company and getting certificate or investment principle permit by applying to the one-stop integrated services.[21]

Access limitations imposed on foreign investment have been justified on economic, social, political or national security grounds. Within this context, BITs negotiations have evolved into two clear models:

Option 1: The "admission clause" model. The admission and establishment is subject to the domestic laws of the host country.

- "The right to be admitted" is entitled to the host state, which frames its model BIT with such admission provisions as "shall admit," and "in accordance with local legislation."

- It allows the host country to apply any admission and screening mechanism for foreign investment that it may have in place and so to determine the conditions under which foreign investment will be allowed to enter the country.

---

[18]   UNCTAD, see http://investmentpolicyhub.unctad.org/IIA.

[19]   *Agreement between The Government of Denmark and The Government of The Republic of Indonesia Concerning The Encouragement and The Reciprocal Protection of Investments,* signed 30 January 1968, [1970] UNTS 224 (entered into force 2 July 1968), Article II(a) ('Denmark–Indonesia BIT').

[20]   Finland–Indonesia BIT.

[21]   Law No 25 of 2007 concerning Investment (Indonesia), Articles 5 and 25(3) ('Indonesian Investment Law')

Option 2: The "right of establishment" model. Foreign investors are granted a right of establishment, although not in an absolute manner.

"The right of establishment" consists of providing foreign investors with NT + MFN treatment, not only once the investment has been established, but also with respect to the establishment (entry).

- Investors of one party will receive treatment with regard to investing in the territory of the other party that is not less favorable
  (i)   than for domestic investors (NT)
  (ii) and investors of any other third country (MFN)
- These treaties are aimed at liberalizing investment flows.

BITs may contain country-specific reservations. In practice no state will grant unlimited access to FDI. However, parties retain some flexibility to control the admission of foreign investment from the other party, usually by allowing for the inclusion of a list of industries, activities, or laws and regulations for which it is not obligated to grant NT and MFN treatment in the pre-establishment phase. The result is that NT and MFN as a principle is subject to clearly stated exceptions (and by definition with limited scope). Use of this approach was traditionally limited to US BITs and later Canada (post-NAFTA); however, over the last decade, this method has been adopted by other nations, such as Japan.

As a result of having these, a growing number of developing countries actually apply two different BIT models, depending on who their treaty partners are. The "admission clause" model is followed mostly in BITs with European countries, whereas the "right of establishment" model is followed mainly in treaties concluded by Canada, Japan, and the United States.

Hypothesis

Pre-establishment is more oriented towards investors.
Admission clause: less oriented towards investors than establishment.

Examples

Option 1: The admission clause

Most BITs admit investors of the other contracting party only if such investments conform to the host country's legislation.

- **Hong Kong, China–Austria BIT (1996)**. Article 2:1: "Each Contracting Party shall encourage and create favorable conditions for investors of the other Contracting Party to make investments in its area, and, *subject to its laws and regulations*, shall admit such investments."

continued on the next page

Continued

- **German model BIT**. Article 2: "*in accordance with its legislation ...*"
- **Japan–Mongolia BIT (2001).** Article 2: "Each Contracting Party shall, subject to its rights to exercise powers *in accordance with the applicable laws and regulations*, encourage and create favorable conditions for investors of the other Contracting Party to make investment in its territory, and, subject to the same rights, shall adroit such investment."

Option 2: The right of establishment clause

- **US–Panama BIT (1982)**. Article 2.1 (one provision for both NT & MFN + pre-establishment):

  "Each Party shall maintain favorable conditions for investment in its territory by nationals and companies of the other Party. Each Party *shall permit and treat such investment, and activities associated therewith*, on a basis no less favorable than that accorded in like situations to investment or associated activities of its own nationals or companies, or of nationals or companies of any third country, whichever is the more favorable ..."

- **Finland-Nigeria BIT (2005).** Two provisions for both NT & MFN + pre-establishment:

  Article 3.1: "Each Contracting Party shall accord to investors of the other Contracting Party and to their investments, a treatment no less favorable than the treatment it accords to its own investors and their investments with respect to the acquisition, expansion, operation, management, maintenance, use, enjoyment and sale or other disposal of investments."

  Article 3.2: "Each Contracting Party shall accord to investors of the other Contracting Party and to their investments, *a treatment no less favorable than the treatment it accords to investors of the most favored nation* and to their investments with respect to the establishment, acquisition, expansion, operation, management, maintenance, use, enjoyment, and sale or other disposal of investments."

- Finland BITs (after 2001) limits pre-establishment NT to the "acquisition" of existing companies, "without expressly" covering the "direct constitution or establishment" of a company; thus arguably allowing solely for mergers and acquisitions and excluding greenfield investments. Acquisition being the main form of foreign investment in a country, we still consider that such a small limitation conducts us to place this kind of BITs in the Option 2 category.

- **Japan–Myanmar BIT (2013).** Article 2: "Each Contracting Party shall in its Area accord to investors of the other Contracting Party and to their investments treatment *no less favorable than the treatment it accords in like circumstances to its own investors and to their investments* with respect to investment activities."

How to use the index:

Our index must reflect this basic binary distinction:
Admission is less expected to encourage a favorable environment for FDI, while right of establishment can be presumed to encourage a favorable environment for FDI.

Admission Clause = Circumscribed = 1.
Right of Establishment = Extensive = 2.

3.3   National Treatment

National treatment (NT) is treatment given by host countries to foreign investors that is at least as favorable as that afforded to domestic investors (Bjorklund 2010). Therefore, it is the most important standard of treatment in IIAs (UNCTAD 1999). Its purpose is to avoid both *de jure* and *de facto* discrimination in foreign investment (Bjorklund 2010). According to Bjorkland, *de jure* discrimination occurs where foreign and domestic investors are treated differently under the laws or policies of host countries, whereas *de facto* discrimination happens because of the different treatment in fact. Under the IIAs, NT is generally indicated by the terms "no less favorable than" and/or "in like circumstances" (Subedi 2012). An example of an NT clause is provided in article 1102 of the NAFTA, which states:

> "Each party shall accord to investors of another party treatment no less favorable than it accords, in like circumstances, to its own investors with respect to the establishment, acquisition, expansion, management, conduct, operation, and sale or other disposition of investments."[22]

However, the scope of NT is difficult to define because definitions of "like circumstances" and "similar circumstances" are not exact (Chaisse 2015a). These circumstances depend on the factual situation of the application of NT and the standard of comparison between the treatment of national and foreign investment (UNCTAD 1999). Hence, three components need to be proved to resolve investment disputes regarding NT claims: (i) comparing among appropriate comparator investors or investment, (ii) examining the difference in treatments received by every comparator, and (iii) considering justifiable factors which cause any difference in treatment (Chaisse 2015a).

As another example in Asia and the Pacific, under Indonesia's old BITs, no special provision was made for national treatment (Chaisse 2015a). However, this situation changed because the investment policy applied by the government focused on the liberalization approach. As a result, more recent Indonesian BITs provide national treatment for foreign investors but contain particular exceptions, such as conditions and protocols.

---

[22]   *The North American Free Trade Agreement*, signed 17 December 1992, 32 ILM 289 and 605 (entered into force 1 January 1994), Chapter 11 ("NAFTA").

The inclusion of a conditional national treatment provision can be found in the BIT between Finland and Indonesia which states:

> "The Government of the Republic of Indonesia, while recognizing the principle of national treatment of investments made by investors of the Republic of Finland in the territory of the Republic of Indonesia, reserves the right to maintain limited exceptions to national treatment. This treatment shall in no case be less favorable than Law No 1 of 1967, as amended in 1970, permits."—Quoted in Chaisse 2015a.

In a nutshell, NT means the obligation of contracting parties to grant investors of the other contracting party treatment no less favorable than the treatment they grant to investments of their own investors.

Hypothesis

The NT provides foreign investors with a guarantee against discrimination which encourage FDI.
It will be very important to establish a link between NT and the choice of admission clause model, or right of establishment.

Examples: Extensive

"Neither Contracting Party shall in its area subject investors of the other Contracting Party, for example as regards their management, maintenance, use, enjoyment or disposal of their investments, to *treatment less favorable than that which it accords to its own investors or to investors of any other State.*" (**Turkey–Israel BIT**)

Some BITs use "non-discriminatory treatment" as a basis to define NT and MFN (as in the **US–Bulgaria BIT**):

"(f) "nondiscriminatory" treatment means treatment that is at least as favorable as the better of *national treatment or most-favored-nation treatment;*

(g) "national treatment" means treatment that is at least as favorable as the most favorable treatment accorded by a Party to companies or nationals of that Party in like circumstances; and

(h) "most-favored-nation treatment" means treatment that is..."

Some BITs refer to both investment and investor first when they define fair and equitable treatment and then only refer to investment when they define NT and/or MFN, or vice-versa (as in the **Russian Federation–Lithuania BIT 1999**):

continued on the next page

Continued

"1. Each Contracting Party shall accord in its territory *to the investors, investments* made by investors of the other Contracting Party and activities related to such investments fair and equal treatment …

2. The treatment, set forth in the paragraph 1 of this Article, shall be at least no less favorable than the treatment accorded by the Contracting Party *to the investments* and activities related to such investments of its own investors or the investors of third state."

Lebanon–Russian Federation BIT (1997) Article 3: Each Contracting Party shall ensure in its territory fair and equitable treatment of *the investments made by investors* of the other Contracting Party and activities … and exclude the use of discriminatory measures …The treatment referred to in paragraph I of this Article shall be at least as favorable as that granted to the investments and activities in connection with such investments by its own investors or investors of third state…

Exceptions to NT: See Limited Scope of MFN (Option 2)

NB: Classical exception on FTAs and customs unions (CU) (virtually all BITs) should not be taken into account (see MFN).

Examples: Circumscribed

Some BITs allow contracting states to have exceptions to NT in its legislation (as in the Russian Federation–Sweden BIT):

"Each contracting Party may have in its legislation *limited exceptions to national treatment* provided for in Para (2) of this Article."

Canada–PRC BIT (2012) Article 5: "Each Contracting Party shall accord to investors of the other Contracting Party treatment no less favorable than that it accords, in like circumstances, to investors of a non-Contracting Party with respect to the establishment, acquisition, expansion, management, conduct, operation and sale or other disposition of investments in its territory" …

Article 8: *"Article 5 does not apply to…"*

How to use the index:

If NT is enshrined in IIA (Extensive) = More oriented towards foreign investors = 2.
If NT is not (or subject to substantive exceptions or unilateral NT) Circumscribed = More oriented towards the host State = 1.

3.4   Most Favored Nation Clause

The MFN treatment is another standard of treatment in order to avoid discrimination in foreign investment. The concept of MFN treatment in investment is that the more favorable treatments provided in recent IIAs concluded by host states are also applied to all other states that have agreed on previous agreements even though no mutual benefit is given by these existing states (Chaisse 2015a). Therefore, the other investments are entitled to the same treatment (Vandevelde 2010).

The MFN standard of treatment is not required under customary law, but was included in all Asian IIAs "to ensure that the relevant parties treat each other in a manner at least as favorable as they treat third parties" (Dolzer and Schreuer 2012). The effect of having the MFN clause is to "widen the rights of the investor," as the material scope of the MFN is open to the contents of future treaties and practices within countries that cannot be foreseen (Dolzer and Schreuer 2012).

Therefore, as Asian IIAs generally provide differing substantive standards of treatment, and even the specific features of each standard may vary, MFN can be a powerful tool to incorporate increased protection via treaty clause importation. Indeed, it has been stated that "it is universally agreed that the very essence of an MFN provision in a BIT is to afford to investors all material protection provided by subsequent treaties."[23]

MFN treatment standard means that investments or investors of one party are entitled to treatment by the other party that is no less favorable than the treatment the latter grants to investments or investors of any other third country.

Applying the MFN Standard: An Example

FET protection can be found in almost all of the Sino-Belt Road Initiative jurisdictions IIAs, although in a few earlier treaties, such as PRC–Bahrain BIT (1999), PRC–Hungary BIT (1991), PRC–Pakistan BIT (1989), and PRC–Poland BIT (1988), the word "fair" is absent and only "equitable treatment" is referred to.[24]

Step 1: Find a Weak FET Clause

ARTICLE 3

1. Investments and activities associated with investments of investors of either Contracting Party Shall be accorded equitable treatment and shall enjoy protection in the territory of the other Contracting Party.

Fair and Equitable Treatment Clause: PRC–Pakistan BIT (1989).

---

[23] *Vladimir Berschader and Moïse Berschader v. The Russian Federation*, SCC Case No. 080/2004. PARA 179.

[24] An FET clause is not provided in the BITs with Belarus or Turkey.

In this example a Chinese investor in Pakistan may find the Fair and Equitable treatment clause to be quite limited. The investor may seek to import stronger protection from another of Pakistan's IIAs.

Step 2: Find the Relevant MFN Clause in the Treaty

ARTICLE 3

1. The treatment and protection … shall not be less favorable than that accorded to investments and activities associated with investments of investors of any third State.

MFN Clause: PRC–Pakistan BIT (1989).

Step 3: Find a Stronger FET Clause in a Third Party Treaty (with the host state)

ARTICLE 2 PROMOTION AND PROTECTION OF INVESTMENT

3. Each Contracting State shall at all times ensure fair and equitable treatment to the investments of investors of the other Contracting State. Each Contracting State shall ensure that the management, maintenance, use, enjoyment, acquisition or disposal of investments or rights related to investment and its associated activities in its territory of investors of the other Contracting State shall not in any way be subjected to or impaired by arbitrary, unreasonable or discriminatory measures.

4.i. Each Contracting State shall endeavor to take the necessary measures and legislations for granting of appropriate facilities, incentives and other forms of encouragement for investments made by investors of the other Contracting State.

4.ii. Investors of either Contracting State shall be entitled to apply to the competent authorities in the host State for the appropriate facilities, incentives and other forms of encouragement and the host State shall grant them all assistance, consents, approvals, licenses and authorizations to such an extent and on such terms and conditions of the host State as shall, from time to time, be determined by the laws and regulations.

Fair and Equitable Treatment Clause: Bahrain–Pakistan BIT (2014).

The investor may look to Pakistan's BIT with Bahrain in 2014 to argue that the equitable treatment must be *fair*: that the "management, maintenance, use, enjoyment, acquisition or disposal of investments" must not be "subjected to or impaired by arbitrary, unreasonable or discriminatory measures"; that the host state "shall endeavor to take the necessary measures and legislations for granting of appropriate facilities, incentives and other forms of encouragement for investments," and that the investor may "apply to the competent authorities in the host State for the appropriate facilities, incentives and other forms of encouragement and the host State shall grant them all assistance, consents, approvals, licenses and authorizations," possible according to its law.

Step 4: Find the Case Law to Support Importation Using the MFN Clause

The Chinese investor can point to a plethora of cases to support their argument.[25] For instance in Rumeli Telekom v. Kazakhstan, where the Kazakh government terminated the Turkish investor's investment contract, the tribunal imported an FET standard into the Turkish–Kazakh BIT from third-party treaties, in particular the United Kingdom–Kazakh BIT.[26] In Bayindir v. Pakistan, where the Turkish investor's highway construction contract was in issue, an International Centre for Settlement of Investment Disputes (ICSID) tribunal authorized the import of the FET clause in the Pakistan–Switzerland BIT (1995) into the Pakistan–Turkey BIT (1995).[27] Furthermore, in White Industries v. India, where the Australian investor had a contract with a state-owned mining entity, the tribunal accepted the import from the India–Kuwait BIT of an obligation to "provide effective means of asserting claims and enforcing rights" into the India–Australia BIT, as claimed by the investor.[28] In ATA v. Jordan, where the Turkish investor had a contract to construct a dike at the Dead Sea, the tribunal applied an MFN clause to import a fair and equitable treatment and treatment no less favorable than that required by international law clause.[29]

- The MFN standard of treatment is not required under customary law, but was included in the Sino-Belt and Road Initiative IIAs, as with other IIAs, "to ensure that the relevant parties treat each other in a manner at least as favorable as they treat third parties" (Dolzer and Schreuer 2012). The effect of having the MFN clause is to "widen the rights of the investor" as the material scope of the MFN is open to the contents of future treaties and state practices that cannot be foreseen.

- Therefore, as the Sino-Belt and Road Initiative BITs generally provide differing substantive standards of treatment, and even the specific features of each standard may vary, MFN can be a powerful tool to incorporate increased protection through treaty clause importation.[30] Indeed, it has been stated that "it is universally agreed that the very essence of an MFN provision in a BIT is to afford to investors all material protection provided by subsequent treaties."[31]

> **Hypothesis**
>
> The MFN standard ensures that investments receive the best treatment that each party has granted to the investments of any other third country.
>
> Therefore, MFN standard establishes, at least in principle, equal treatment for all foreign investors.

---

[25] Cases include *Pope & Talbot Inc. v. Canada*, Award on the Merits of Phase 2, 10 April 2001, 7 ICSID Rep. 102 (UNCITRAL 2001); Award in Respect of Damages, 31 May 2002, 7 ICSID Rep. 148 (UNCITRAL 2002); *ADF Group, Inc. v. United States*, Final Award, 9 January 2003, 6 ICSID Rep. 470 (W. Bank 2003); *MTD Equity Sdn. Bhd. v. Chile*, Award, 25 May 2004, 12 ICSID Rep. 6 (W. Bank 2004); *CMS Gas Transmission Company v. The Argentine Republic*, ICSID, ARB/01/8, award of 12 May 2005.

[26] *Rumeli Telekom A.S. v. Kazakhstan*, ICSID Case No. ARB/05/16, Award, 29 July 2008.

[27] *Bayindir Insaat Turizm Ticaret Ve Sanayi AS v. Islamic Republic of Pakistan*, ICSID. ARB/03/29, Decision on Jurisdiction of 14 November 2005.

[28] *White Industries Australia Limited v. Republic of India*, UNCITRAL, award of 30 November 2011.

[29] *ATA Construction, Industrial and Trading Company v. Hashemite Kingdom of Jordan*, ICSID Case No. ARB/08/2, Award, 18 May 2010 at 16.

[30] Although a handful of new treaties (in particular those signed by the European Union and India) carefully carve out the scope of the MFN clause, the remaining thousands (including all Chinese ones) of existing treaties do not limit the scope of the MFN clause.

[31] *Vladimir Berschader and Moïse Berschader v. The Russian Federation*, SCC Case No. 080/2004. PARA 179.

Examples

Option 1: Extensive MFN

Another less common approach makes reference to "all matters" or "all areas" covered by the IIA.

Article 4 Treatment Argentina–Spain BIT (1991) "In *all matters* subject to this Agreement, this treatment shall be no less favorable than that extended by each Party to the investments made in its territory by investors of a third country." (This provision of the Argentina-Spain BIT led the tribunal in the *Maffezini vs. Spain case*)

Classical exception for free trade agreements (FTAs) virtually all BITs (does not affect the categorization of MFN):

- BITs *commonly* provide that MFN treatment shall not apply, so as to require that investors be given the same benefits as may be given to investors under the terms of customs unions, free trade zones, economic unions, and the like. **This provision ensures that the BIT does not become an impediment to regional economic integration.**

- **Hong Kong, China–Austria BIT (1996)**. Article 4: MFN obligations shall not apply, so as to require the host state to match any benefits resulting from any arrangements "designed to lead in future" to a regional customs, monetary, tariff, or trade arrangement, or from any arrangement with any third state in the region "designed to promote regional cooperation in the economic, social, labor, industrial or monetary fields within the framework of specific projects."

- **Japan–Switzerland EPA (2009)**, for instance, establishes that the MFN clause does not apply to third treaties, providing for substantial liberalization of investment; where such liberalization occurs, it would be subject to consultation to incorporate it into the base treaty. In Article 88.3, the Most-Favored-Nation Treatment provision, says: "If a Party accords more favorable treatment to investors of a non-Party and their investments by concluding or amending a free trade agreement, customs union or similar agreement that provides for substantial liberalization of investment, it shall not be obliged to accord such treatment to investors of the other Party and their investments. Any such treatment accorded by a Party shall be notified to the other Party without delay and the former Party shall endeavor to accord to investors of the latter Party and their investments treatment no less favorable than that accorded under the concluded or amended agreement. The former Party, upon request by the latter Party, shall enter into negotiations with a view to incorporating into this Agreement treatment no less favorable than that accorded under such concluded or amended agreement."

continued on the next page

Continued

Option 2: Limited scope of MFN

Does the MFN apply to the investment only (and not the investor)?

Some BITs provide that MFN treatment applies only to investment. For example, BITs between the PRC on the one hand, and Cambodia, Qatar, and Brunei Darussalam, respectively, on the other hand: Some of the earlier PRC BITs are limited in scope and cover only investments in their MFN clause, without direct reference to "investment-related activities" (see the PRC–Sweden BIT 1982).

Australia–Uruguay BIT (2001). Article 4, Most favored nation provision: "Each Party shall at all times treat *investments* in its own territory on a basis no less favorable than that accorded to investments of investors of any third country..."

Some IIAs cover only investments and there may be measures affecting the investor but not the investment (for example, a discriminatory entry or operational barrier applicable only to foreigners). This would have the consequence of excluding foreign individuals or companies from the MFN standard and limiting it to subsidiaries constituted or assets acquired under the legislation of the host state. This has been a common approach for countries like the PRC and Australia.

India–Latvia BIT (2010). Article 4: "[T]he provisions of paragraph (1) and (2) above shall not be construed so as to oblige one Contracting Party to extend to the investors of the other Contracting Party and to their investments and returns on investments the present or future benefit of any treatment, preference or privilege resulting from..."

How to use the index:

**An extensive MFN is more favorable to FDI environment = 2.
No MFN[32] or MFN subject to conditions may not be that favorable to FDI environment (limited set of activities and/or investor not covered) = 1.**

3.5   Expropriation and Indirect Expropriation

Expropriation is governed by provisions in every IIA because taking control of foreign-owned assets is the most serious impairment that governments in host countries can create (Dolzer and Schreuer 2012). Lowenfeld (2008) pointed out that host countries are able to expropriate according to four conditions: where taking ownership is in the public interest; involves no discrimination; is conducted in accordance with legal process; and "prompt, adequate, and effective" payment is made as compensation. There are two types of foreign investment expropriation. The first type is a direct expropriation, which happens because the government directly takes possession of foreign

---

[32]   MFN treatment has become a core principle of BITs. Only 5% of existing treaties do not have an MFN clause.

investors' assets (Chaisse 2015a). However, nowadays, this action has been decreasing because countries do not want to put their investment climate at risk by nationalizing foreign assets (Dolzer and Schreuer 2012). Moreover, imposing direct expropriation damages a country's reputation (Dolzer and Schreuer 2012).

The second form of expropriation is an indirect expropriation. This is where action taken by the country destroys the economic benefit of foreign investors (Vandevelde 2010). In this regard, foreign investors may still own their assets but their value falls because of a state's regulatory actions, such as taking away management control or and ruling that depreciate the value of assets (Vandevelde 2010). However, not all regulatory actions that reduce the value of investment are regarded as indirect expropriations. This makes it important, within the context of an IIAQ, to identify and classify actions that are indirect expropriations (Vandevelde 2010).

Another example is given by expropriation provisions in all of Indonesia's BITs, where expropriation is allowed when there is a public purpose, in accordance with process of law, adequate compensation is provided. According to one of Indonesia's BITs:

> A party shall not nationalize, expropriate or subject to measure having effect equivalent to nationalization or expropriation (hereinafter referred to as "expropriation") the investments of investors of the other party unless the following conditions are complied with: (a) the expropriation is for a public purpose related to the internal needs of the Party and under due process of law; (b) the expropriation is non-discriminatory; and (c) the expropriation is accompanied by the payment of prompt, adequate and effective compensation.[33]

However, the scope of expropriation in all Indonesia's BITs covers only direct expropriation. They offer no formulation about indirect expropriation (Knorich and Berger 2014).

Hypothesis

Most BITs contain brief and general **indirect** expropriation provisions which focus on the effect of the government action. But some IIAs do not protect investors against **indirect** expropriation.

Examples: Indirect Expropriation

Treaties that France has entered into refer to "measures of expropriation or nationalization or any other measures the effect of which would be direct or indirect dispossession." The UK treaties provide that expropriation also covers measures "having effect equivalent to nationalization or expropriation."

continued on the next page

---

[33]   Australia–Indonesia BIT, Article VI(1).

Continued

Other treaties, such as some of those concluded by Sweden, refer to "any direct or indirect measure" or "any other measure having the same nature or the same effect against investments."

The former United States model BIT mentions "measures tantamount to expropriation or nationalization." Several United States treaties are more specific on these measures: "any other measure or series of measures, direct or indirect, tantamount to expropriation (including the levying of taxation, the compulsory sale of all or part of an investment, or the impairment or deprivation of its management, control of economic value ...".

Although the specific wording may vary, most expropriation clauses have continued with the traditional approach of extending protection to host country measures that may have an effect equivalent to expropriation or are tantamount to expropriation (other agreements use the term indirect expropriations). Examples include:

Bahrain–Mexico BIT (2012) Article 6: "Neither Contracting Party may expropriate or nationalize an investment either directly or indirectly through measures tantamount to expropriation or nationalization ("expropriation"), except ..."

Bangladesh–Viet Nam BIT (2005) Article 5: Neither of the Contracting Parties shall take any measures of expropriation, nationalization or any dispossession, having effect equivalent to nationalization or expropriation against the investment of investors of the other Contracting Party, except under the following conditions...

Absence of Indirect Expropriation

Italy does not cover indirect expropriation in any of the BITs, while the UK deals with indirect expropriation in only one out of seven treaties.

How to use the index:

If direct AND indirect expropriation are covered; the provision is more favorable to FDI environment = 2.
If indirect expropriation is not covered = 1.

3.6   Fair and Equitable Treatment

Fair and equitable treatment is one of absolute standards of treatment in foreign investment so that it is contained in most of IIAs both bilateral investment treaties and preferential trade agreements (Yannaca-Small 2010). It requires equality between foreign and domestic investors in particular circumstances, such as getting access to national courts and agencies, and imposing taxes and dealing with domestic regulations (Lowenfeld 2008). However, in practice, the scope of the fair and equitable treatment standard is subject to debate. Some argue that this standard is derived from customary international law, while others claim it is a supplement to general international law (Dolzer and Schreuer 2012).

Moreover, some formulations in the IIAs are proven by the distinction of treaty language in defining this standard (Kalicki and Medeiros 2007). Some treaties are formed by referencing the fair and equitable treatment standard with customary international law, while the others do not include international law in the formulation (Kalicki and Medeiros 2007).

One of the IIAs with a formulation that this standard is in conjunction with customary international law is NAFTA. Under this agreement, Canada, Mexico, and the United States have agreed to accord "treatment in accordance with international law, including fair and equitable treatment and full protection and security."[34] Due to the variation of treaty language, it can be proven that the definition of the fair and equitable treatment standard is extensive and its determination relies on the particular circumstances in each investment case (Dolzer and Schreuer 2012).

The agreement between Australia and the People's Republic of China on the Reciprocal Encouragement and Protection of Investments (referred to as the Australia–PRC BIT) contains a FET clause. Article 3 (a) says:

> "A Contracting Party shall at all times:
> (a) ensure fair and equitable treatment in its own territory to investments and activities associated with such investments."[35]

The FET clause in the Australia–PRC BIT is in plain language. Given that the bilateral investment treaty is not qualified in any way, the FET clause can be explained through interpretation of different tribunal awards. Tribunals have interpreted the meaning of the FET standard in many different ways. *EDF v. Romania Award* observed no consensus among International Centre for Settlement of Investment Disputes (ICSID) tribunals on the meaning of fair and equitable treatment.[36] In that case, the tribunal expressed the view that investing parties consider one of the main components of the FET standard to be legitimate and reasonable expectations, an opinion supported by other tribunals (footnote 35). This position is further supported by the case of *Waste Management v. Mexico*, whereby the Tribunal stated that: "In applying this standard [i.e., the FET], it is relevant that the treatment is in breach of representations made by the host state which were reasonably relied on by the claimant."[37] In the case of *British Caribbean Bank v. Belize Award*, the tribunal noted that the aspect of protection of investments afforded under the FET standard has resisted formulation of an all-inclusive definition.[38] To the contrary, the matter of *Lemire v. Ukraine* considered that FET is a "term of art, and any effort to decipher the ordinary meaning of the words used only leads to analogous terms of almost equal vagueness."[39]

---

[34] NAFTA Article 1105.

[35] Agreement between the Government of Australia and the Government of the People's Republic of China on the Reciprocal Encouragement and Protection of Investments, Australia-PRC, signed on 11 July 1988, (entered into force 11 July 1988), Article 3 (a).

[36] *EDF (Services) Limited v. Romania (UK v. Romania) (Award) (2009)* ICSID Case No. ARB/05/13, 215.

[37] *Waste Management, Inc. v. Mexico (US v. Mexico) (Number 2—Final Award) (2004)* ICSID Case No. ARB (AF)/00/3 (NAFTA), 98.

[38] *British Caribbean Bank Ltd. v. Government of Belize (UK v. Belize) (Award) (2014)* PCA Case No. 2010-18/BCB-BZ, 281.

[39] *Joseph C. Lemire v. Ukraine (US v. Ukraine) (Decision on Jurisdiction and Liability) (2010)* ICSID Case No. ARB/06/18, 258.

In a contrasting view, the tribunal in the case of *CME v. Czech* gave the FET clause in the Netherlands-Czech Republic BIT an extensive meaning.[40] The tribunal found that the Czech Government had contravened its treaty obligation of providing the FET clause and that it, as the "Respondent State," had acted in an inequitable manner.[41] Notably, legal proceedings brought by the owner of CME, Ronald S. Lauder, at the same time as the tribunal returned a finding that no violation of the same standard had occurred, despite the same facts.[42] However, the Lauder ruling observed that the FET clause "related to the traditional standard of due diligence and provides a minimum international standard that forms part of customary international law" (footnote 41). The Lauder ruling went one step further and made reference that the context of the BITs standard is subjective and dependent upon the factual context (footnote 41). As a result, the FET standard "will also provide discrimination against the beneficiary of the standard, where discrimination would amount to unfairness or inequity in the circumstances" (Kalicki and Medeiros 2007).

At present, no registered ICSID arbitrations and, more notably, the FET standard have taken place in relation the Australia–PRC BIT (Clifford Chance 2015). Given that the decisions from other tribunals are not binding, there is an evident lack in predictability of what a tribunal would find should a FET claim be lodged by an Australia and/or PRC foreign investor under the BIT. Furthermore, it would be dependent upon the tribunal who heard the claim. Current arbitral practice demonstrates that a host government's conduct—including its legislative, administrative, and judicial conduct—has potential to be found in breach of the FET standard. Such a finding would benefit a foreign investor who chose to initiate a claim under the FET clause of the Australia–PRC BIT.[43] At present, it is uncertain how an arbitral tribunal would interpret the FET clause under the Australia–PRC BIT.

Another example is provided by Indonesia's BITs, most of which cover the fair and equitable treatment in foreign investment. As one of the early BITs in Indonesia, the 1977 treaty with the United Kingdom stated that:

> investments of nationals or companies of either Contracting Party shall at all times be accorded fair and equitable treatment and shall enjoy full protection and security in the territory of the other Contracting Party...[44]

Meanwhile, in some more recent Indonesia's BITs, there is also an inclusion of the fair and equitable treatment: "Each Contracting Party shall in its territory accord to investments and returns of investments of investors of the other Contracting Party fair and equitable treatment and full protection and security."[45] However, the BIT between Indonesia and Morocco governs that the fair and equitable treatment is "subject to strictly necessary measures to maintain public order."[46]

---

[40] *CME v. Czech Republic (Netherlands v. Czech Republic) (Partial Award)* (2001) UNCITRAL Case, 611-612; Kalicki, Jean and Suzana Medeiros 2007.

[41] *CME v. Czech Republic (Netherlands v. Czech Republic) (Partial Award)* (2001) UNCITRAL Case, 611-612.

[42] *Ronald S. Lauder v. Czech Republic (US v. Czech Republic) (Final Award)* (2001) UNCITRAL Case, 293.

[43] Kalicki, Jean and Suzana Medeiros, 'Fair, Equitable and Ambiguous: What is Fair and Equitable Treatment in International Investment Law?' (2007) 22 ICSID Review 218.

[44] *Agreement between the Government of the United Kingdom of Great Britain and Northern Ireland and the Government of the Republic of Indonesia for the Promotion and Protection of Investments, signed 27 April 1976, (1977) Treaty Series 62, (entered into force 24 March 1977), Article 3(2) ('The UK–Indonesia BIT').*

[45] Finland–Indonesia BIT, Article 2(2).

[46] Indonesia–Morocco BIT, Article II(2).

The following observations can be drawn from this survey:

- BITs usually include one or several general principles intended to provide overall criteria by which to judge whether the treatment given to an investment is satisfactory.

- Fair and equitable treatment (FET) is the most important (in theory and practice) of those general principles.

- Clauses providing foreign investment with FET are widespread in IIAs:

  (i) German Model Investment Protection Treaty: "Each Contracting State shall … accord investments by investors … fair and equitable treatment as well as full protection under the Treaty."

  (ii) The provisions lack sufficient clarity. They are not totally new, but have been applied extensively only since 2000.

Hypothesis

FET offers high protection but is not present in all treaties.
FET encourages a more favorable environment for FDI flows, while no FET might be less encouraging to FDI.

Examples

- In **Australia–Hungary BIT (1991)**. FET is in article 3:2: "A Contracting Party shall ensure fair and equitable treatment in its own territory to investments."

- **Macedonia–Kazakhstan BIT (2012)**. Article 2: "Each Party shall provide to investments and returns of investments of investors of either Party fair and equitable treatment, and also full protection …"

- **Romania–Kazakhstan BIT (2010)**. Article 3: "Each Contracting Party shall ensure fair and equitable treatment within its territory to investments of the investors of the other Contracting Party …"

If such a provision is absent (i.e., no mention is made of *fair, fairness, equitable, equity*), it means that FET is not considered.

That said, IIAs without an FET clause are rarely found today.

How to use the index:

If FET is enshrined in IIA = More favorable to FDI environment = 2.
If FET is not = Less favorable to FDI environment = 1.

3.7   Transfer of Investment-related Funds Out of Host State

The clauses on transfer payments are considered by investors and the host country as the most important in a bilateral treaty. They deal with one aspect of the relationship between the host country and the foreign investor on which their interests can diverge widely.[47]

Whereas such clauses can and do differ from treaty to treaty, most IIAs stipulate that a wide range of payments and other investment-related funds shall have a right to be transferred out of the host state without delay, and, typically, in a freely convertible currency. A comprehensive agreement would normally cover (i) "returns" on investment, including all profits, benefits, interest, capital gains, royalties, and fees (such as for management, technical assistance, or other functions); (ii) proceeds from the liquidation or sale of all or any part of the investment; and (iii) payments under a contract, and earnings of other remuneration to foreigner personnel in connection with the investment.

Some IIAs permit deviation from obligations enshrined in the transfer of funds provision in four cases.[48] Whereas this is most common in FTAs, which usually allow safeguards motivated by the balance of payments or external financial difficulties,[49] exceptions are rather unusual in bilateral investment agreements. One should assume that an extensive guarantee to allow outward transfers is likely to attract FDI, whereas exceptions have to be considered as relatively less encouraging to FDI. Indeed, from the foreign investors' point of view, these clauses are key in investment treaties, as the ability to freely repatriate funds can be important in making investment decisions.

- Views on this provision diverge significantly between developing and developed countries (Poulsen 2010, p.110).

- While such clauses differ from treaty to treaty, most BITs stipulate that a wide range of payments and other-investment related funds shall have a right to be transferred out of the host state without delay and, typically, in a freely convertible currency.

- The many investment claims brought against Argentina after the 2001 financial crisis sparked debate about the risks of not subjecting such guarantees to certain exceptions. While this particular crisis might have brought attention, the issue has always been controversial. Jeswald Salacuse stated: "[T]he negotiation of BIT provisions on monetary transfer is often one of the most difficult negotiations to conclude. Capital-exporting countries seek extensive, unrestricted guarantees on monetary transfers, while developing countries press for limited guarantees, subject to a variety of exceptions."[50]

---

[47]   The numerous investment claims brought against Argentina in the wake of its 2001 financial crisis have sparked a debate on the risks of not subjecting such guarantees to certain exceptions. But while this particular crisis might have brought attention to this issue, it has always been controversial. See Salacuse (2013), Williams (2001), and Naon (1996).

[48]   One option is to subject the transfer clause to domestic laws, in which case the host state is free to limit the flow of capital out of its economy, for instance during economic crises, as long as it is done through law. For example, the *Agreement for the Promotion and Mutual Protection of Investments*, Portugal–Bulgaria, Article 5, 27 May 1993. Another option is to allow exceptions to the free transfer of funds, but only during balance-of-payments difficulties and typically with a requirement that such restrictions should be necessary, non-discriminatory, and temporary. See for example, the *Agreement for the Promotion and Protection of Investments, UK–Argentina*, Article 6, 11 December 1990. Finally, some treaties include other major limitations that permit restrictions on capital flight, such as certain Chilean BITs attempting to restrict short-term capital in- and outflows. See, for example, *Agreement for the Promotion and Reciprocal Protection of Investments*, Chile–Austria, protocol, 8 September 1999. Other possible exception: the host state should be able to prevent foreign investors from freely transferring revenue and capital out of its country if it were under economic difficulties.

[49]   See, for instance, Republic of Korea–Singapore FTA, Article 10.12, or NAFTA, Article 21.04.

[50]   Salacuse, J. W. 1990. BIT by BIT: The Growth of Bilateral Investment Treaties and Their Impact on Foreign Investment in Developing Countries. *The International Lawyer*. 24 (3). Fall 1990. pp. 655–75.

Hypothesis

From a foreign investor point of view, these clauses are key in investment treaties, as the ability to freely repatriate funds can be an important factor in investment decisions. Developing countries, on the other hand, often have an interest in not restraining their ability to adopt certain restrictive exchange rates or other measures to prevent or confront economic and financial crises.

If extensive free transfer of investment-related funds out of the host state is ensured by the IIA = More favorable to FDI environment = 2.

If subject to conditions = Less favorable or unclear effect on FDI environment = 1.

Examples

Option 1:

Hong Kong, China–Austria BIT (1996) provides for a relatively extensive one (Article 7.1: "unrestricted right to transfer extensive their investments [...] and returns" + "Investors shall also have the unrestricted right to transfer extensive **in particular, but not exclusively**...]. And Article 7.2: "Transfers of currency shall be effected without delay in any freely convertible currency".

Austria–India BIT (1999) Article 6 has different wording but similar meaning.

Option 2: (Seven suboptions)

- One option is to subject the transfer clause to domestic laws, in which case the host state is free to limit the flow of capital out of its economy, for instance during economic crises, as long as it is done through law. An example is the Agreement for the Promotion and Mutual Protection of Investments in the **Portugal–Bulgaria BIT (1993)**.

- Another option is to allow exceptions to the free transfer of funds, but only during balance-of-payments difficulties, and typically with a requirement that such restrictions should be necessary, non-discriminatory, and temporary. An example is the Agreement for the Promotion and Protection of Investments in the **UK–Argentina BIT (1990)**.

- Finally, some treaties include other major limitations that permit restrictions on capital flight, such as certain Chilean BITs attempting to restrict short-term capital flows in and out of the country. An example is the Agreement for the Promotion and Reciprocal Protection of Investments in the **Chile–Austria BIT (1999)**.

continued on the next page

Continued

- Other possible exception: A host state should be able to prevent foreign investors from freely transferring revenue and capital out of its country if the economy is facing difficulties.

- Protocol of **Netherlands–Chile BIT 1998**: *"Chile* retains the right to allow the repatriation of capital only after one year has elapsed from the date it was brought in by the national." Only *Chile* unilaterally restricts short-term capital inflows and outflows. This provision may not be favorable for *Chile* FDI flows but *not affect the Netherlands* FDI flows. But we classify such treaty as restrictive to FDI flows.

- A series of tiny but cumbersome conditions (such as in the **Belize–Netherlands BIT 2002**): "A Contracting Party *may delay the transfer* through the equitable, non-discriminatory and good faith application of measures, (a) to protect the **rights of creditors**, or (b) relating to or ensuring compliance with laws and regulations:

  (i) on the **issuing, trading** and dealing in **securities, futures and derivatives**,

  (ii) concerning **reports or records of transfers**,

  (iii) in connection with **criminal offences and orders of judgements** in administrative and adjudicatory proceedings."

Japan–Israel BIT (2017). Article 14: "Notwithstanding paragraphs 1 and 2, a Contracting Party may delay or prevent a transfer through the equitable, non-discriminatory and good-faith application of its laws and regulations."

- Refer to MFN and national laws (as in **the Bulgaria–Poland BIT**): *"In accordance with the legal regulations* of either Contracting Party all transfer subject to this Article shall be accorded treatment no less favorable than that accorded to the transfer of investments made by an investor of any third State."

India–Nepal BIT (2011). Article 7: "Each Contracting Party shall, in accordance with its laws, permit all funds of an investor of the other Contracting Party related to an investment in its territory to be freely transferred, without unreasonable delay and on a non-discriminatory basis ..."

How to use the index:

There is an extensive free transfer of investment provision: More favorable to FDI environment = 2.
There is no such clause (illustrated by one of the seven suboptions): Less favorable to FDI environment = 1.

3.8 Noneconomic Standards

Here we should consider if any protection is offered to noneconomic standards (be they environmental, labor, or other significant attributes). Most of the time standards for these are not included.

Hypothesis

IIAs grant strong protections to investors of either state party who are operating in the territory of the other party and may impinge upon human rights enforcement and realization in several ways. The investment treaty regime must be reformed to take better account of the human rights regime, ameliorating situations in which states face conflicting international legal obligations under the two regimes.

As a result, an IIA without any such provision may be considered as generally being more favorable to FDI environment while an IIA with any provision seeking to protect human rights may be considered as having a neutral effect or being less favorable to FDI environment. This approach in the codification does not suggest in any way that policy makers should avoid regulating non-economic matters in IIAs.

Examples

Strong Protection (Category 1 in ADB IIA Tool Kit)

In the **Austria BIT Model**:

Article 4 (environment): "The Contracting Parties recognize that it is inappropriate to encourage investment by weakening or reducing the protections afforded in domestic environmental laws. Accordingly, each Party shall strive to ensure that it does not waive or otherwise derogate from, or offer to waive or otherwise derogate from, such laws in a manner that weakens or reduces the protections afforded in those laws as an encouragement for the establishment, acquisition, expansion, or retention of an investment in its territory. If a Party considers that the other Party has offered such an encouragement, it may request consultations with the other Party and the two Parties shall consult with a view to avoiding any such encouragement."

Article 5 (labor): "The Parties recognize that it is inappropriate to encourage investment by weakening or reducing the protections afforded in domestic labor laws. Accordingly, each Party shall strive to ensure that it does not waive or otherwise derogate from, or offer to waive or otherwise derogate from, such laws in a manner that weakens or reduces adherence to the internationally recognized labor rights referred to in paragraph 2 as an encouragement for the establishment, acquisition, expansion, or retention of an investment in its territory.

continued on the next page

Continued

"(2) For the purposes of this Article, 'labor laws' means each Party's statutes or regulations, that are directly related to the following internationally recognized labor rights:
(a) the right of association;
(b) the right to organize and to bargain collectively;
(c) a prohibition on the use of any form of forced or compulsory labour;
(d) labor protections for children and young people, including a minimum age for the employment of children and the prohibition and elimination of the worst forms of child labor, and
(e) acceptable conditions of work with respect to minimum wages, hours of work, and occupational safety and health."

Japan–Iraq BIT (2012).

Article 22 (labor and health): "Each Contracting Party recognizes that it is inappropriate to encourage investment by investors of the other Contracting Party and of a non-Contracting Party by relaxing its health, safety or environmental measures, or by lowering its labor standards. To this effect each Contracting Party should not waive or otherwise derogate from such measures and standards as an encouragement for the establishment, acquisition or expansion of investments in its Area by investors of the other Contracting Party and of a non-Contracting Party."

Austria- Kazakhstan BIT (2010).

Article 4 (investment and environment): "The Parties do not encourage an investment by weakening the requirements of its national legislation in the field of environment."

Article 5 (labor laws): "(1) The Parties do not encourage an investment by weakening the requirements of its national legislation in the field of labor.

(2) For the purposes of this Article, national legislation in the field of labor is directly related to the following internationally recognized labor rights."

Weak or no protection of noneconomic standards illustrated by many examples (category 2 in ADB IIA Tool Kit):

The **Hong Kong, China–Austria BIT (1996)** makes no provision of this kind at all.

In the **Norway BIT Model,** such concerns are reflected in a provision that reads:

"The Parties recognize that it is inappropriate to encourage investment by relaxing domestic health, safety or environmental measures or core labour standards. Accordingly, a Party should not waive or otherwise derogate from, or offer to waive or otherwise derogate from, such measures as an encouragement for the establishment, acquisition, expansion or retention of an investment of an investor."

continued on the next page

Continued

In the **Finland BIT Model**, the preamble (not binding) says: "Contracting parties *agreeing* that these objectives can be achieved *without relaxing* health, safety and environmental measures of general application." The model does not use the words *recognizing* or *considering*.

That form is used in the **Netherlands–Dominican Republic (2006) BIT**, where the preamble says: "*Recognizing* that the development of economic and business ties will promote internationally accepted labor standards **(not enforceable)**; *Considering* that these objectives can be achieved without undermining policies with respect to health, social security and the environment; **(not enforceable)**"

In **Germany–India BIT (1995)**. Article 12: "Nothing in this Agreement prevent either Contracting Party from applying prohibitions or restriction to the extent necessary for the protection of its essential security interests, or for the prevention of diseases in animals or plants."

The "security interests" in the Germany-India BIT do not cover noneconomic standards and the "prevention of diseases in animals and plants" reference is too small to be considered as having negative impact on FDI. As a result, for this BIT, the index = 2, as shown below.

How to use the index:

If there is no mention of noneconomic standards (such as for human rights, environmental protection, and health), or only in the preamble, the IIA is favorable to high FDI flows = 2.

If there is such a mention, it is less favorable = 1.

3.9   Public Interest Obligations

Due to the system of private international governance, some arbitrators are effectively striking down national regulations, which could have consequences on state's sovereignty and so threaten the public interest.[51] National regulations involving environmental safety and human rights should be defined by states without external interventions from non-state actors or international bodies. Furthermore, arbitrators within the system of private international governance also impose threats on democracy of a nation as democracy is usually characterized by accountability and public participation.

Public interest has long been defined as the interest of the state and its constituents (Black's Law Dictionary 2004). States have the duty act in their own and their citizens' best interests, which

---

[51] For example, see Choudhury, B. 2008. Recapturing Public Power: Is Investment Arbitration's Engagement of the Public Interest Contributing to the Democratic Deficit? *Vand. J. Transnat'l L.* 41. 775.

usually takes in issues such as environmental concerns or human rights. Problems arise when regulating for the public interest interferes with investment agreements, which might result as violations of national, most favored nation, or fair and equitable treatment provisions. Further issues emerge once the public service sector is bound by trade and investment obligations. In short, it is possible for investment arbitration to create problems for citizens' basic and most essential rights.

- From the perspective of sustainable development, many IIAs include labor, health, and environmental standards in order to avoid investor–state disputes post-establishment, while some IIAs only include standards without stipulating obligations for investors' compliance. Other IIAs also include the obligation of investors to perform within the standards.

Hypothesis

IIAs with public interest obligations clauses have more restrictive effects on investors. Therefore, IIAs which include such a clause may be less favorable to FDI environment.

IIAs without such a clause are generally more favorable to FDI environment.

Examples

Option 1:

Morocco–Nigeria BIT (2016). Article 18 (Post-establishment obligations):

"(1) Investments shall, in keeping with good practice requirements relating to the size and nature of the investment, maintain an environmental management system. Companies in areas of resource exploitation and high-risk industrial enterprises shall maintain a current certification to ISO 14001 or an equivalent environmental management standard.

(2) Investors and investments shall uphold human rights in the host state.

(3) Investors and investments shall act in accordance with core labor standards as required by the ILO [International Labour Organization] Declaration on Fundamental Principles and Rights of Work, 1998.

(4) Investors and investments shall not manage or operate the investments in a manner that circumvents international environmental, labor and human rights obligations to which the host state and/or home state are Parties."

Option 2:

Most BITs do not include such a clause.

> **How to use the index:**
>
> **If there is no such clause: favorable to FDI = 2.**
> **If there is such a clause: less favorable to FDI = 1.**

3.10   The Umbrella Clause

Some IIAs cover only disputes which relate to an "obligation under this agreement"—i.e., only for claims of BIT violations. Others extend the jurisdiction to "any dispute relating to investments." Others IIAs create an obligation under international law for a host state to, for example, "observe any obligation it may have entered to ... constantly guarantee the observance of the commitments it has entered into [and] ... observe any obligation it has assumed," along with other formulations in respect to investments. These provisions are commonly called *"umbrella clauses."* An umbrella clause can be drafted in different ways. Under the Germany–Pakistan BIT, Article 7 reads:

> *"Either Party shall observe any other obligation it may have entered into with regard to investments by nationals or companies of the other party."*

In the Singapore–Czech Republic BIT 1995, Article 7.2 states:

> *"Each Contracting Party shall observe commitments, additional to those specified in this Agreement it has entered in to with respect to investments of the investors of the other Contracting Party. Each Contracting Party shall not interfere with any commitments, additional to those specified in this Agreement, entered into by nationals or companies with the nationals or companies of the other Contracting Party as regards their investments."*

In essence, an umbrella clause extends the scope of the application of a BIT and offers the investor more protection.

We should make the distinction between IIAs with an umbrella clause and those that do not give the investor and investment such favorable protection. An umbrella clause extends the scope of application of BIT because it offers more protection to the foreign investor. Inclusion of an umbrella clause is a positive sign which we hypothesize will be an incentive to invest. Conversely, if there is no such umbrella clause, there will be less interest to use a BIT to invest.

Some BITs cover only disputes relating to an "obligation under this agreement"—i.e., only for claims of BIT violations. Others extend the jurisdiction to "any dispute relating to investments." Other BITs create an international law obligation that a host state shall, for example, "observe any obligation it may have entered," or "constantly guarantee the observance of the commitments it has entered into," or "observe any obligation it has assumed," and other wording to that effect in respect to investments.

Of note, whereas Switzerland, the Netherlands, the United Kingdom, and Germany often include umbrella clauses in their BITs, they are included only in a minority of BITs involving France, Australia, and Japan.

Hypothesis

An umbrella clause extends the scope of application of an IIA. It offers more protection to foreign investors. If umbrella clause is included, it is expected to encourage a more favorable environment for FDI flows..

If umbrella clause is not included, it is expected to encourage a less favorable environment for FDI flows.

Examples

Germany–Pakistan BIT (1959). "Either Party shall observe any other obligation it may have entered into with regard to investments by nationals or companies of the other party."

Australia–Poland BIT (1991). "A Contracting Party shall, subject to its law, do all in its power to ensure that a written undertaking given by a competent authority to a national of the other Contracting Party with regard to an investment is respected."

Singapore–Czech Republic BIT (1995). "Each Contracting Party shall observe commitments, additional to those specified in this Agreement it has entered in to with respect to investments of the investors of the other Contracting Party. Each Contracting Party shall not interfere with any commitments, additional to those specified in this Agreement, entered into by nationals or companies with the nationals or companies of the other Contracting Party as regards their investments."

Kyrgyz Republic–Kuwait BIT (2015). Article 13: "If the national legislation of the State of either Contracting Party or obligations under international law existing at present or established hereafter between the Contracting Parties, in addition to this Agreement, contain rules, whether general or specific, entitling investments by investors of the other Contracting Party to a treatment more favorable than is provided for by this Agreement, such rules shall to the extent that they are more favorable to the investor prevail over this Agreement."

Some BITs require the Contracting Parties to observe their obligations under "*contracts,*" "*special agreements,*" and so on. That is favorable to FDI.

Austria–Kyrgyz Republic BIT (2016). Article 11: "Each Contracting Party shall observe any obligation it may have entered into with regard to specific investments by investors of the other Contracting Party. This means, inter alia, that the breach of a contract between the investor and the host State will amount to a violation of this treaty."

However, if some BITs limit the scope of a special agreement, such as only in the area of nature resources, it should be Circumscribed.

> **How to use the index:**
>
> **No umbrella clause = Circumscribed = 1.**
> **Presence of umbrella clause = Extensive = 2.**

3.11 Temporal Scope of Application

On the issue of application through time, two main questions have traditionally arisen in BIT negotiations. First, whether treaty protection should be extended to investments made before the entry into force of the agreement. The second issue relates to the determination of the period of application of the agreement: its duration and termination (its "life").

Hypothesis

If coverage is restricted to the future, protection under the IIA will be extended to investments made before the IIA comes into force. This kind of clause will have a positive effect on investors.

Otherwise, the absence of such a clause is negative for investors.

Examples

Option 1:

Austria–Hong Kong, China BIT(1996). Article 11: Does the BIT apply "to all investments whether made before or after the date of its entry into force."

Colombia–PRC BIT (2008). Article 11: "This Agreement is applicable to existing investments at the time of its entry into force, as well as to investments made thereafter in the territory of a Contracting Party in accordance with the law of the latter by investors of the other Contracting Party. However, this Agreement only applies to disputes arisen after the Agreement enters into force."

Option 2:

Application only to investment made after or no mention of the temporal application would have been marked as circumscribed.

> **How to use the index:**
>
> **IIA applies to investment done after = Circumscribed = 1.**
> **IIA applies to investments before and after = Extensive = 2.**

3.12   Performance Requirements

States use performance requirements (PRs) widely to achieve several goals. PR is an instrument to protect certain industries. It can also be an instrument for implementing regional development policies. PR may cause a state to violate its World Trade Organization (WTO) obligations under the Agreement on Trade-Related Investment Measures (TRIMs). Therefore, more prohibitions of PR in IIAs have recently taken effect. That noted, PR can be effective (i) if evidence suggests that some PRs have helped a number of countries meet different development objectives, and (ii) a state has sufficient capacity to implement them and monitor impact. In the past decades, PRs were not on the upswing.

> **Hypothesis**
>
> IIAs without PR prohibitions will make the case go to WTO rather than arbitration. The absence of such clause is less favorable to FDI environment.
>
> For IIAs which include PR prohibitions, the content and scope of PR can be categorized into two kinds:
>
> 1) TRIMs reference,
> 2) TRIMs+ prohibited in IIAs.
>
> Because only a few IIAs include a PR clause, no matter which type of PR clause an IIA has, we suppose the clause will be more favorable to FDI environment.

> **Examples**
>
> **Option 1: IIAs without PR prohibitions**
>
> **Brazil–Colombia BIT (2015)**, **Mexico–United Arab Emirates BIT (2016)**, and **Azerbaijan–San Marino BIT (2015)**. There are no prohibitions on PRs for these agreements.
>
> *continued on the next page*

Continued

Option 2: TRIMs prohibited (TRIMs reference)

PRC–Republic of Korea FTA (2015). Article 12.7, Prohibition of Performance Requirements:

"1. The provisions of the Agreement on Trade-Related Investment Measures in Annex 1A to WTO Agreement are incorporated into and made part of this Chapter, *mutatis mutandis* and shall apply with respect to all covered investments under this Chapter.

2. Neither Party shall, in its territory, impose unreasonable or discriminatory measures on covered investment by investors of the other Party concerning performance requirements on export or transfer of technology."

Option 3: TRIMs + prohibited (listed prohibition)

Japan–Lao People's Democratic Republic BIT (2008). Article 7, Prohibition of Performance Requirements:

"1. Neither Contracting Party shall impose or enforce, as a condition for investment activities in its Area of an investor of the other Contracting Party, any of the following requirements:

    (a) to export a given level or percentage of goods or services;

    (b) to achieve a given level or percentage of domestic content;

    (c) to purchase, use or accord a preference to goods produced or services provided in its Area, or to purchase goods or services from natural or legal persons or any other entity in its Area;

    (d) to relate in any way the volume or value of imports to the volume or value of exports or to the amount of foreign exchange inflows associated with investments of that investor;

    (e) to restrict sales of goods or services in its Area that investments of that investor produce or provide by relating such sales in any way to the volume or value of its exports or foreign exchange earnings;

    (f) to appoint, as executives, managers or members of boards of directors, individuals of any particular nationality;

    (g) to transfer technology, a production process or other proprietary knowledge to a natural or legal person or any other entity in its Area, except when the requirement:

    •   is imposed or enforced by a court, administrative tribunal or competition authority to remedy an alleged violation of competition laws; or

    •   concerns the transfer of intellectual property rights which is undertaken in a manner not inconsistent with the Agreement on Trade-Related Aspects of Intellectual Property Rights in Annex 1C to the WTO Agreement (hereinafter referred to as "the TRIPS Agreement");

continued on the next page

Continued

> (h) to locate the headquarters of that investor for a specific region or the world market in its Area;
>
> (i) to hire a given number or percentage of its nationals;
>
> (j) to achieve a given level or value of research and development in its Area; or
>
> (k) to supply one or more of the goods that the investor produces or the services that the investor provides to a specific region or the world market, exclusively from the Area of the former Contracting Party.
>
> 2. The provisions of paragraph 1 above do not preclude either Contracting Party from conditioning the receipt or continued receipt of an advantage, in connection with investment activities in its Area of an investor of the other Contracting Party, on compliance with any of the requirements set forth in paragraph 1 (g) through (k) above."
>
> **Option 4: PR clause included in treatment of investment clause**
>
> **Republic of Korea-El Salvador BIT (1998)**. Article 3, Treatment of the Investments: "… (4) Neither of the Contracting Parties can impose nor oblige the fulfillment of the following requirements or compromises, in relation to any investment in its territory: (a) export a determined type, level or percentage of goods or services, in general terms or toward a specific market …"

How to use the index:

If there is no prohibition of PRs: less favorable to FDI environment = 1.
If there is PR prohibition: more favorable to FDI environment = 2.

3.13   The Exception Clause

More and more BITs contain an exception clause that includes several scenarios. Generally speaking, the exception clause can be divided into two categories: **security** exceptions and **general exceptions.**

National security interests are important both for developed and developing counties. Security exceptions are practiced by developed countries to protect strategic industries, and by developing countries in times of economic turmoil or crisis.

The most famous general exceptions clause is GATT Article XX. Some IIAs just incorporate the WTO general exceptions clause. Other IIAs take inspiration from WTO general exceptions clause.

An exception clause in an IIA prevents the state from violating the treaty, rather than removing the responsibility after its violation.

Hypothesis

If the exception clause is in an IIA = less favorable to FDI environment = 1.
If such a clause is absent in an IIA = more favorable to FDI environment =2.

Examples

Option 1: Security exceptions included

Japan–Lao People's Democratic Republic BIT (2008). Article 18, General and Security Exceptions:

"1.   Notwithstanding any other provisions in this Agreement other than the provisions of Article 13, each Contracting Party may:
   (a) take any measures which it considers necessary for the protection of its essential security interests; …"

Japan–Iran BIT (2016). Article 13, General and Security Exceptions …

Option 2: General exceptions included

Canada–Guinea BIT (2015): There is only general exceptions clause in BIT, without exception clause.

Canada–PRC BIT (2012). Article 33: General exceptions of the BIT.

Option 3: Exception clauses covering other BIT provisions

Other exceptions may be included in the BIT aiming at specific provisions. However, these exceptions do not include exceptions for MFN, NT, and the free transfer of investment-related funds.

Option 4: An exception clause is not included

Morocco-Rwanda BIT (2016), Austria-Kyrgyz Republic BIT (2016), and the Bangladesh-Denmark BIT (2009).

How to use the index:

There is an exception clause: not favorable more favorable to FDI environment = 1.
There is no such clause: more favorable to FDI environment = 2.

3.14   Access to Arbitration

Every IIA needs a dispute settlement provision to resolve investment claims. One of the dispute settlement mechanisms is arbitration. In investment deals, parties can choose to settle investment disputes through either the International Centre for Settlement of Investment Disputes (ICSID) or another type of arbitration, such as institutional and ad hoc arbitration (Lowenfeld 2008). If parties decide to resolve disputes through the ICSID, they must give consent to arbitration according to requirements under article 25 (1) of the *ICSID Convention*, in which this consent cannot be withdrawn, and moreover, the arbitration rules are applied in accordance with this Convention (Lowenfeld 2008). However, if parties select the other type of arbitration, then different rules, such as those under the United Nations Commission on International Trade Law (UNCITRAL) or the New York Convention, are applied (Lowenfeld 2008). Mostly, the reference of arbitration in IIAs is arbitration under the ICSID if both capital-exporting states and host countries are signatories to the ICSID Convention (Lowenfeld 2008).

Indonesia's BITs are examples of how access to arbitration works, as each includes a dispute settlement provision. The provision covers mechanisms applied to settle investment claims brought by foreign investors against the host state. Generally, the first step taken to resolve disputes is through amicable processes, such as diplomatic channels,[52] consultation, and negotiation.[53] The further step if parties cannot settle those claims is through arbitration through the bodies mentioned above. Most of Indonesia's BITs stipulate that when the parties fail to settle amicably, the dispute settlement mechanism applied by contracting parties is arbitration by the ICSID.[54]

In sum, BITs include general provisions on investor–state dispute settlement that specify the different arbitration venues available to the investor, the procedures for appointing arbitrators, and the obligation for contracting parties to consider the arbitration award as final and binding, and that provide for enforcement of the award in their respective territories.

This mechanism ensures that the dispute is decided on legal grounds, separating it from political considerations. The first clause of an investor–state dispute settlement provision typically defines the types of disputes to which the mechanisms apply.

Hypothesis

An investor–state dispute is an incentive to invest since it provides access to international (neutral) jurisdiction as an ultimate resort.

If such a mechanism is in the IIA = positive effect = 2.
If subject to conditions = doubtful effect = 1.

---

[52]   See Denmark–Indonesia BIT, article VIII (1).

[53]   See Finland–Indonesia BIT, article 9(1); *Agreement between the Government of the Republic Indonesia and the Government of the Republic of Uzbekistan concerning the Promotion and Protection of Investment, signed 27 August 1996* (entered into force 27 April 1997), article VIII(1) ("Indonesia–Uzbekistan BIT").

[54]   See the UK-Indonesia BIT, article 7(1); Finland-Indonesia BIT, article 9(2)(b); Indonesia-Uzbekistan BIT, article VIII(3); Singapore-Indonesia BIT, article VIII(2)(c).

Examples

Option 1: Investor-state dispute settlement without conditions

Austria–Hong Kong, China BIT(1996): Article 9 provides for a relatively extensive scope of application of investor–state dispute settlement procedures without any condition: "any dispute … concerning an investment." This approach is by far the most common.

Option 2: No investor-state dispute, or a mechanism with conditions

PRC–Barbados BIT (1998). Condition possible: Foreign investors must refer the dispute to an administrative review procedure according to domestic law in the first place, and if the dispute still exists 3 months after the investor has brought the issue to the review procedure, he can submit the dispute to international arbitration.

Colombia–Japan BIT (2011). Article 27: "With regard to the submission of a claim to arbitration by a disputing investor, the disputing Party may require, subject to its laws and regulations, that local administrative remedies shall be exhausted in advance…"

Condition possible: If the issue has been brought before a court in the PRC, investors must be able to withdraw the case according to domestic law. Otherwise, they cannot submit the dispute to international arbitration. This rule of so-called "fork in the road" requires the investor to make a choice between submission to a domestic court or to international arbitration, and where, once made, the choice is final and irreversible.

Condition possible: Some BITs require investors to wait almost 1 year (as in the **Netherlands–Romania BIT (1994)**: "In case the dispute is not resolved pursuant to paragraph 2(a) within a period of 10 months the investor may, subject to withdrawing his claim from the courts of the Contracting Party concerned, submit the dispute to arbitration under paragraph 2b or c."

Option 3: Unilateral provision

PRC–Germany BIT (2003)

"With respect to investments in the People's Republic of China, an investor of the Federal Republic of Germany may submit a dispute for arbitration under the following conditions only."

Example 1: Find a Weak Dispute Resolution Procedure

Article 8 Settlement of Investment Disputes

(1) Disputes or differences between one Contracting State and an investor of the other Contracting State concerning an investment of that investor in the territory and maritime zones of the former Contracting State shall, if possible, be settled amicably.

(2) If such disputes or differences cannot be settled according to the provisions of Paragraph (1) of this Article within a period of six months from the date either party requested amicable settlement and the parties have not agreed to any other dispute settlement procedures, the investor concerned may choose one or both of the following means of resolutions: (a) file complaint with and seek relief from the competent administrative authority or agency of the Contracting State in whose territory or maritime zones the investment was made; (b) file suit with the competent court of law of the Contracting State in whose territory or maritime zones the investment was made.

(3) The dispute relating to the amount of compensation and any other dispute agreed upon by both parties may be submitted to an international Arbitral Tribunal.

Dispute Resolution Procedure in the **PRC–Kuwait BIT (1985).**

In this example, a PRC investor in Kuwait may find the dispute resolution procedure to be quite limited. The investor may seek to import more advantage dispute resolution procedure from another of Kuwait's IIAs.

Example 2: Find a Stronger Dispute Resolution Procedure

Article 16 Settlement of Investment Disputes between a Contracting Party and an Investor of the Other Contracting Party

3. Any investment dispute shall, as far as possible, be settled amicably through consultations between the disputing investor and the disputing Party (hereinafter referred to in this Article as "the disputing parties").

4. If the investment dispute cannot be settled through such consultations within three months from the date on which the disputing investor requested in writing the disputing Party for consultations, the disputing investor may, subject to subparagraph 7(a), submit the investment dispute to one of the following international conciliations or arbitrations:

   (a) conciliation or arbitration in accordance with the Convention on the Settlement of Investment Disputes between States and Nationals of Other States, done at Washington, March 18, 1965 (hereinafter referred to in this Article as "the ICSID Convention"), so long as the ICSID Convention is in force between the Contracting Parties;

continued on the next page

Continued

    (b) conciliation or arbitration under the Additional Facility Rules of the International Centre for Settlement of Investment Disputes, so long as the ICSID Convention is not in force between the Contracting Parties;

    (c) arbitration under the Arbitration Rules of the United Nations Commission on International Trade Law, adopted by the United Nations Commission on International Trade Law on April 28, 1976; and

    (d) if agreed with the disputing Party, any arbitration in accordance with other arbitration rules.

Dispute Resolution Procedure in the **Kuwait–Japan BIT (2014)**.

How to use the index:

If there is an investor-state dispute provision: favorable to FDI environment = 2.
If there is no such clause or unilateral provision: less favorable to FDI environment = 1.

3.15   Transparency in Investor–State Arbitration

As mentioned earlier, IIAs may or may not include general provisions for investor–state dispute settlement. The hypothesis and examples are in the previous statement. Here are the more detailed and categorized types. The two types of Investor–State Dispute Mechanisms (ISDMs) in IIAs introduced below are based on the existence of the mechanism in the IIA.

- ISDM Provision: In some BITs, issues relating to ISDM are covered in general provisions. These may include procedures for appointing arbitrators, the obligations of contracting parties, the enforcement of awards, and so on.

- ISDM Transparency: As the transparency of ISDM gets increasing attention, more IIAs make specific provision for mechanisms that deal with this issue.

Hypothesis

ISDM specifications on transparency mechanisms such as stipulations on public arbitration hearings, grant more protection to either party. However, by themselves, ISDM provisions may not have as strong a positive impact on FDI.

Examples

Option 1: ISDM specification of transparency mechanisms

Hong Kong, China–Canada BIT (2016).

Article 23, Submission of a Claim to Arbitration:

"3. ...The Parties shall promptly publish the supplemental rules of procedure that they adopt or otherwise make them available to interested persons."

Article 27, Documents to, and Participation of, the Non-Respondent Party:

"1. The UNCITRAL Transparency Rules shall apply with respect to the participation of the non-respondent Party in arbitration proceedings under this Section except as modified by this Agreement.

2. The respondent Party shall deliver to the non-respondent Party a copy of the notice of intent to submit a claim to arbitration and other documents submitted along with such notice within 30 days of the date those documents have been delivered to the respondent Party. The non- respondent Party is entitled, upon request and at its cost, to receive from the respondent Party a copy of the evidence that has been tendered to the Tribunal, copies of pleadings filed in the arbitration, and the written argument of the disputing parties. The non-respondent Party receiving such information shall treat the information as if it were the respondent Party.

3. The non-respondent Party may make oral and written submissions to a Tribunal only on questions of interpretation of this Agreement and has the right to attend hearings held under this Section."

Article 29 Transparency of Proceedings:

"1. The UNCITRAL Transparency Rules shall apply in connection with proceedings under this Section except as modified by this Agreement.

2. Subject to Article 7 of the UNCITRAL Transparency Rules:

    (a) the notice of intent and the decision on arbitrator challenge shall be included in the list of documents referred to in Article 3(1) of the UNCITRAL Transparency Rules; and

    (b) exhibits shall be included in the list of documents referred to in Article 3(2) of the UNCITRAL Transparency Rules.

3. Notwithstanding Article 2 of the UNCITRAL Transparency Rules, prior to the constitution of the Tribunal, the respondent Party shall make publicly available in a timely manner relevant documents pursuant to paragraph 2, subject to the redaction of confidential information. Such documentation may be made publicly available by communication to the repository referred to in Article 8 of the UNCITRAL Transparency Rules.

4. A disputing party may disclose to other persons in connection with the arbitral proceedings, including witnesses and experts, such unredacted documents as it

continued on the next page

Continued

considers necessary in the course of proceedings under this Section. However, the disputing party shall ensure that those persons protect the confidential information in those documents as directed by the Tribunal.

5. A Party may share with government officials and sub-national government officials, if applicable, such unredacted documents as it considers necessary in the course of proceedings under this Section. However, such Party shall ensure that those persons protect the confidential information in those documents as directed by the Tribunal.

6. To the extent that a Tribunal's confidentiality order designates information as confidential and a Party's law on access to information requires public access to that information, the Party's law on access to information shall prevail. However, a Party shall endeavor to apply its law on access to information so as to protect information designated confidential by the Tribunal."

Option 2: An investor-state dispute mechanism provision

Japan–Kenya BIT (2016). Article 14 Settlement of Disputes Between the Contracting Parties: general provision including ISDS, scope and consent, forums but without transparency.

Bangladesh–Denmark BIT (2009) and many other BITs do not include the transparency of ISDS either.

How to use the index:

If there is ISDM provision: less favorable to FDI environment = 1.
If there is ISDM specification of transparency: more favorable to FDI environment = 2.

4. Using the Index

The coding of thousands of treaties and provisions in the ADB IIA Tool Kit supports numerous avenues for research in the universe of IIAs. The Tool Kit allows any researcher to more easily identify major trends in investment agreements in Asia, while assisting in identifying exceptions or unusual patterns that require a more detailed study. The Tool Kit aims to provide a breakthrough for looking at all these issues with a new eye. This section presents examples of possible applications of the Tool Kit, the take up of which can encourage development of further applications to meet the needs of researchers and policymakers.

The ADB IIA Tool Kit introduces two major levels of information. It enables the gathering of data on a great number of IIAs at the provision level and the agreement level.

4.1 Provision-Level Indicators

The provision-level indicators allow precise analysis of specific provisions. For instance, a large number of definitions of the concept of investment can be extracted and compared across specific countries, regions, and over time to identify trends and changing patterns. The provision-level also brings attention to the specific meaning and likely impact of each provision by grouping them in indicators that hone in on key specificities of IIAs. For instance, instead of simply comparing the definitions of National Treatment, one can look at the liberalization indicator of a treaty or series of treaties; part (1) of the following explanation. It is also possible to identify the degree of anti-discrimination (2), as well as other indicators (3).

4.1.1. ADB IIA Tool Kit Liberalization Quality Indicator

Most IIAs require that, subject to their domestic laws, parties shall encourage and admit into their territories investments by nationals and companies of the other party (UNCTAD 2007). The reference to domestic laws means that the commitment to encourage foreign investment is subject to existing or future restrictions on the entry of foreign investment contained in domestic legislation. The priority accorded in these IIAs to domestic laws reflects the fact that these treaties have been designed primarily to regulate the treatment of foreign investment after admission. A fundamentally different approach to the admission of foreign investment is found in most IIAs concluded by the United States.[55] These require the application of MFN and NT with respect both to admission and to subsequent treatment of investments, subject however to the right of each party to make or maintain exceptions in sectors or matters specified in an annex to the IIA.

---

[55] BITs that include liberalization provisions are mostly North American and Japanese. In fact, the inclusion of investment liberalization provisions in the US and Japanese BITs originates in earlier trade and investment agreements within FCNs, whereas in the post-war period, the US' FCNs embodied liberalization provisions based on NT and MFN treatment. See Vandevelde (2005).

The ADB IIA Tool Kit Liberalization Quality Indicator has been created on the basis of the coding of three provisions: (i) the regulation of foreign investment entry (in the form of an admission clause or pre-establishment rights), (ii) the regulation of transfer of investment-related funds out of the host state, and (iii) the presence of noneconomic standards. The Liberalization Quality Indicator provides a measure of the degree of openness of an economy to foreign investment, or, conversely, the degree of control that a state maintains over foreign investment.

To calculate the "ADB IIA Tool Kit Liberalization Quality Indicator," one needs to extract from the ADB IIA Tool Kit the sum of the regulation of foreign investment entry (in the form of admission clauses or pre-establishment rights), the regulation of transfer of investment-related funds out of the host state, and, finally, the presence of noneconomic standards. The higher the indicator (closer to 2), the more open the local economy. The lower the indicator (closer to 1), the more controls on foreign investment are in place.

Table 1 extracts the ADB IIA Tool Kit liberalization indicators for three sample countries (the PRC, Germany, and India). These are chosen as examples because of their different approaches toward inward and outward foreign investment policies.

Table 1: Liberalization Quality Indicator: People's Republic of China, Germany, and India

International Investment Agreements (by country pairs)	ADB IIA Tool Kit Liberalization Quality Indicator (extensive indicator = 1.5-2; circumscribed indicator = 1-1.5)
PRC-Singapore, Madagascar-PRC, New Zealand-PRC, Sri Lanka-PRC	1.00
Belize-PRC, Benin-Germany, Bosnia and Herzegovina-PRC, Brunei Darussalam-PRC, Bulgaria-PRC, Cambodia-PRC, Chile-Germany, Chile-PRC, PRC-Albania, PRC-Argentina, PRC-Australia, PRC-Bahrain, PRC-Benin, PRC-Bolivia, PRC-Botswana, PRC-Colombia, PRC-Costa Rica, PRC-Cote D'Ivoire, PRC-Cuba, PRC-Denmark, PRC-Djibouti, PRC-Ecuador, PRC-Egypt, PRC-Estonia, PRC-Ethiopia, PRC-Georgia, PRC-Ghana, PRC-Greece, PRC-Guyana, PRC-Iceland, PRC-Iran, PRC-Jamaica, PRC-Japan, PRC-Democratic People's Republic of Korea, PRC-Republic of Korea, PRC-Latvia, PRC-Lebanon, PRC-Lithuania, PRC-Mexico, PRC-Norway, PRC-Pakistan, PRC-Peru, PRC-Poland, PRC-Qatar, PRC-Slovakia, PRC-Sweden, PRC-Switzerland, PRC-Turkey, PRC-Uganda, PRC-Uruguay, Croatia-PRC, Czech Republic-PRC, Germany-Bulgaria, Germany-Democratic Republic of the Congo, Germany-Saint Lucia, Germany-Trinidad and Tobago, Greece-Germany, Hungary-PRC, Iceland-India, India-Israel, India-Mexico, India-Syrian Arab Republic, Indonesia-PRC, Iran-Germany, Italy-PRC, Republic of Korea-Germany, Kuwait-PRC, Lao PDR-PRC, Lesotho-Germany, Malaysia-India, Mexico-Germany, Mongolia-PRC, Morocco-PRC, Myanmar-PRC, Papua New Guinea-Germany, Philippines-PRC, Poland-Germany, Portugal-PRC, Romania-PRC, Rwanda-Germany, Senegal-Germany, Slovakia-India, Slovenia-PRC, Spain-PRC, Swaziland-Germany, Swaziland-PRC, Syria-Germany, Thailand-PRC, Trinidad and Tobago-PRC, Uganda-Germany, UK-PRC, Viet Nam-PRC, Viet Nam-Germany, Zimbabwe-Germany	1.33

IIA = international investment agreement, Lao PDR = Lao People's Democratic Republic, PRC = People's Republic of China, UK = United Kingdom.
Source: ADB International Investment Agreements Tool Kit.

A cursory look at Table 1 brings out an array of observations and offers a rich canvas for further analysis. Two main points are highlighted:

- First, among these three countries, the liberalization indicator shows that the People's Republic of China (PRC) is the country with the less liberalized IIAs. Indeed, four of its IIAs (concluded with Singapore, Madagascar, New Zealand, and Sri Lanka) obtain a relatively low score. This may partly be explained by the fact that these IIAs were concluded by the PRC at a time when the country would not export much capital and they reflect a more defensive approach toward foreign investors. The PRC places most of its IIAs in the second category, but only five agreements in the most liberal category.

- Second, in terms of research, the liberalization indicator provides useful information to explore the response of FDI flows to crises, due to, among other factors, current account imbalances. As FDI involves a number of capital transfers (like equity, reinvested earnings or profit shifting), future analyses may account for policies related to long-term capital movements, where FDI are included, besides indicators related to movements of short-term capital such as portfolio investment. Also, the indicator could be applied to explore, for example, questions related to investment liberalization and economic growth.

A comparison of the estimated Liberalization Quality Indicator for all countries in the ADB database is available in Annex II (Figure a).

4.1.2   ADB IIA Tool Kit Anti-discrimination Quality Indicator

MFN treatment and NT are key principles of international investment law. They are expressions, and variations, of the idea of equality, equal treatment, and non-discrimination. Economically, they seek to bring about equal treatment and fair conditions of competition for products which have different origins. The Anti-discrimination Quality Indicator logically combines the coding of these two principles to gauge the degree to which IIAs ensure a certain degree of equality for foreigners (among themselves and/or with regard to nationals). In order to calculate the Anti-discrimination Quality Indicator, we extract and average the values of MFN and NT provisions.

Table 2 extracts the Anti-discrimination Quality Indicator with a view to distinguish treaty practices of five sample countries: the PRC, India, and Indonesia.

In Table 2, the Anti-discrimination Quality Indicator offers useful information at a glance. Two main observations from the data collected are:

- First, and surprisingly, India scores relatively high in the Anti-discrimination indicator. India, except in its IIA with Taipei,China, seems to always provide and require relatively high protection on discrimination. This consistent practice contrasts with the Liberalization Quality Indicator, for which rather inconsistent practice is apparent. This result may partly explain why India has faced many investment claims before international tribunals in recent years. The high degree of protection provided in its IIAs may well generate this greater exposure to treaty claims.

- Second, competition policy has many facets on the national and international level. Yet many analyses neglect the impact of international treaties on the degree of competition and the nature of conditions for equal treatment between domestic and foreign competitors. As mergers and acquisitions are important for foreign investors' market entry, there are questions related to welfare effects for the host country from the actions of foreign firms subject to restricted competition. The Anti-discrimination Quality Indicator provides a way to include the international level, besides supranational policies (like the EU Competition Policy) and domestic policies.

Table 2. ADB IIA Tool Kit Anti-discrimination Quality Indicator: People's Republic of China, India, and Indonesia

International Investment Agreements (by country pairs)	ADB IIA Tool Kit Anti-Discrimination Quality Indicator (circumscribed indicator = 1–1.4; extensive indicator = 1.5–2)
Belize-PRC, Bosnia and Herzegovina-PRC, Brunei Darussalam-PRC, Bulgaria-PRC, Cambodia-PRC, Chile-PRC, PRC-Albania, PRC-Argentina, PRC-Australia, PRC-Bahrain, PRC-Benin, PRC-Bolivia, PRC-Botswana, PRC-Colombia, PRC-Costa Rica, PRC-Cote D'Ivoire, PRC-Cuba, PRC-Denmark, PRC-Djibouti, PRC-Ecuador, PRC-Egypt, PRC-Estonia, PRC-Ethiopia, PRC-Georgia, PRC-Ghana, PRC-Greece, PRC-Guyana, PRC-Iceland, PRC-Iran, PRC-Jamaica, PRC-Japan, PRC-Democratic People's Republic of Korea, PRC-Republic of Korea, PRC-Latvia, PRC-Lebanon, PRC-Lithuania, PRC-Mexico, PRC-Norway, PRC-Pakistan, PRC-Peru, PRC-Poland, PRC-Qatar, PRC-Slovakia, PRC-Sweden, PRC-Switzerland, PRC-Turkey, PRC-Uganda, PRC-Uruguay, Croatia-PRC, Czech Republic-PRC, Hungary-PRC, Indonesia-PRC, Italy-PRC, Kuwait-PRC, Lao PDR-PRC, Mongolia-PRC, Morocco-PRC, Myanmar-PRC, Philippines-PRC, Portugal-PRC, Romania-PRC, Slovenia-PRC, Spain-PRC, Swaziland-PRC, Thailand-PRC, Trinidad and Tobago-PRC, UK-PRC, Viet Nam-PRC	1.33
Indonesia-Croatia, Indonesia-Finland, Indonesia-PRC, Indonesia-India.	1.50
Austria-India, Bangladesh-India, Cyprus-India, Czech Republic-India, France-India, Germany-India, Greece-India, Iceland-India, India-Argentina, India-Armenia, India-Australia, India-Bahrain, India-Belarus, India-Belgium, India-Bosnia and Herzegovina, India-Brunei Darussalam, India-Bulgaria, India-PRC, India-Croatia, India-Denmark, India-Egypt, India-Finland, India-Hungary, India-Israel, India-Jordan, India-Kazakhstan, India-Kyrgyz Republic, India-Latvia, India-Mexico, India-Mongolia, India-Mozambique, India-Oman, India-Qatar, India-Romania, India-Russian Federation, India-Saudi Arabia, India-Republic of Korea, India-Spain, India-Sweden, India-Switzerland, India-Syrian Arab Republic, India-Tajikistan, India-Thailand, India-Trinidad and Tobago, India-UK, India-Viet Nam, India-Yemen, Indonesia-India, Italy-India, Italy-Russian Federation, Kuwait-India, Lao PDR-India, Libya-India, Lithuania-India, Macedonia-India, Malaysia-India, Mauritius-India, Morocco-India, Myanmar-India, Netherlands-India, Philippines-India, Poland-India, Portugal-India, Russian Federation-Egypt, Russian Federation-Hungary, Russian Federation-Japan, Russian Federation-Lithuania, Rwanda-US, Senegal-India, Serbia-India, Slovakia-India, Sri Lanka-India, Sudan-India, Turkey-India, Turkmenistan-India, UK-Russian Federation, Ukraine-India, US-Bulgaria, US-Poland, US-Uruguay, Uzbekistan-India	2.00

IIA = international investment agreement, Lao PDR = Lao People's Democratic Republic, PRC = People's Republic of China, UK = United Kingdom, US = United States.
Source: ADB International Investment Agreements Tool Kit.

A comparison of the estimated Anti-discrimination Quality Indicator for all countries is available in Annex II (Figure b).

4.1.3   Other ADB IIA Tool Kit Quality Indicators

As explained above, the ADB IIA Tool Kit provides coding for the definitions of three key elements which determine the scope of each treaty: the definition of investment, the temporal scope of application, and the umbrella clause. The combination of these elements results in what we have called the "ADB IIA Tool Kit Breadth Quality Indicator." This indicator provides a precise view for each IIA's potential scope of application. The more extensive the scope, the greater is the number of investments protected, and the more important other provisions become. In order to calculate the "ADB IIA Tool Kit Breadth Quality Indicator," one needs to extract from the ADB IIA Tool Kit the sum of the definition of investment, the temporal scope of application, and the umbrella clause. Because each of these codes is equal to 1 or 2, their sum can vary only between 3 and 6. A Breadth Quality Indicator close to 6 indicates that the IIA has a rather extensive scope of application. A result close to 3 indicates the IIA scope of application is rather circumscribed. A comparison of the estimated Breadth Quality Indicator for all countries in the ADB database is available in Annex II (Figure c).

An investor's investment decision is not made on the basis of the legal situation in a given host state at the time of the investment alone, but also accounts for the expectation that the investor will be treated, in the future, fairly and equitably and will not suffer expropriation without compensation. The ADB IIA Tool Kit Regulatory Constraint Quality Indicator provides a precise view of the degree to which foreign investments are protected by IIAs. It does this by combining the score of expropriation and FET provisions into a single score. The closer the sum is to 4, the greater the guard and protection offered to foreign investment. Conversely, the lower the result, the weaker the guard. A comparison of the estimated Regulatory Constraint Indicator for all countries in the ADB database is available in Annex II (Figure d).

Finally, the ADB IIA Tool Kit ISDS Quality Indicator represents the *average across ISDS provisions for all IIAs of a particular country or country group in force.* An investor–state dispute mechanism is an incentive to invest because it provides, as an ultimate resort, access to international (neutral) jurisdiction. In the ADB IIA Tool Kit, if such a mechanism is included in an IIA, it can be expected to have a positive effect on FDI flows. The effect is reduced if the IIA is subject to conditions.[56] In order to calculate the ISDS Quality Indicator, one has to extract the value given to ISDS clause. This is directly used without further calculation as the score of the indicator. The closer the result is to 2, the greater is the access to investor–state arbitration facilitated and offered to foreign investment. Conversely, the lower the result, the more cumbersome is the reliance on arbitration and, hence, the capability to seek the enforcement of the other IIA provisions. A comparison of the estimated ISDS Quality Indicator for all countries in the ADB database is available in Annex II (Figure e).

A synopsis of the indicators estimated with tabulated provisions is presented in Table 3.

---

[56]   The ISDS procedures can, however, be subject to conditions. Possible condition: Foreign investors must refer the dispute to an administrative review procedure according to domestic law in the first place, and if the dispute still exists 3 months after the investor has brought the issue to the review procedure, he can submit the dispute to international arbitration. Possible condition: If the issue has been brought to a court in the PRC, investors must be able to withdraw the case according to domestic law. Otherwise, they cannot submit the dispute to international arbitration. This rule of so-called "fork in the road" requires the investor to choose between submission to a domestic court or to international arbitration, and where the choice once made becomes final and irreversible. See Weeramantry (2012).

Table 3: Summary of Provision-Level Indicators

Indicator	Definition
Liberalization	[Admission vs. Establishment + Transfer funds + Noneconomic Standards]/3
Anti-Discrimination	[Most Favored Nation + National_Treatment]/2
Breadth Quality	Definition of Investment + Temporal Scope + Umbrella Clause
Regulatory Constraint	Fair and Equitable Treatment + Expropriation
ISDS Quality	Access to Arbitration

ISDS = investor–state dispute settlement.
Source: ADB International Investment Agreements Tool Kit.

4.2   Agreement-Level Indicators

The ADB IIA Tool Kit also allows researchers to reanalyze the large volume of IIAs by comparing some indicators in agreements. In a nutshell, the idea is to identify a specific value attached to the investment treaty in order to compare two or more agreements across countries, regions, level of economic development or time period. As examples, we review in this section the ADB IIA Tool Kit quality indicator (in part 1 below), the indicator of heterogeneity (2), and introduce the concept of modulation of coefficients as another refinement to allow full flexibility in the analysis (3).

4.2.1   ADB IIA Tool Kit Quality Indicator: Average

The provision-level indicators provide a finer view of each IIA key components. It is however useful to also look at the broader picture for a sense of the general degree to which a given IIA (or many countries' IIAs) regulate foreign investment. In order to address this need, the ADB IIA Tool Kit quality indicator has been created to represent the average protection provided by an IIA, i.e., the average value of all the 15 key provisions.[57] Such a general indicator allows the comparison of a great number of IIAs; for instance the IIAs of two countries, two groups of countries or even a series of IIAs by generation concluded by a single state.

We have applied this indicator to countries with a great number of IIAs in order to see whether the PRC, Egypt, and India, three emerging economies with well-established practices for treaty negotiations, have had comparable approaches toward the drafting. In addition, we include two of the most advanced economies (Germany and the United States) for comparison.

---

[57]   A certain number does not give information, whether two countries have the *same* provisions or *different* provisions, as different combinations could still lead to the same overall number.

Table 4: ADB IIA Tool Kit Quality Indicator: Argentina, Egypt, Germany, India, and United States

Economy Pairs	ADB IIA Tool Kit Quality Indicator: Average (Low Quality Indicator =1 or close to 1; High Quality Indicator = 2 or close to 2)
Egypt–Belgium–Luxembourg, Egypt-Bulgaria, Egypt-Canada, Egypt-Cyprus, Egypt-Macedonia, FYR, Egypt-Poland, Egypt-Sweden, Egypt-Turkey, Finland-Egypt, Germany-Democratic Republic of the Congo, Germany-Pakistan, Jordan-Egypt, Lebanon-Armenia, Rwanda-Germany	1.55
Argentina-Armenia, Argentina-Bulgaria, Argentina-Netherlands, Argentina-Philippines, Australia-Argentina, Canada-Argentina, Chile-Egypt, Croatia-Albania, Egypt-Australia, Egypt-Belarus, Egypt-Botswana, Egypt-Georgia, Egypt-Kazakhstan, Egypt-Pakistan, Egypt-Romania, Egypt-Turkmenistan, Egypt-Uganda, Egypt-Ukraine, El Salvador-US, Germany-Cameroon, Germany-Bulgaria, Ghana-Egypt, Greece-Argentina, Greece-Germany, Iceland-India, Indonesia-Egypt, Jamaica-Argentina, Japan-Egypt, Jordan-US, Malaysia-Egypt, Malaysia-Germany, Romania-US, Rwanda-US, Senegal-Germany, Singapore-Germany, Syria-Germany, US-Armenia, US-Bahrain, US-Bulgaria, US-Egypt, US-Haiti, US-Kazakhstan, US-Mongolia, US-Nicaragua, US-Panama, US-Poland, US-Russian Federation, Viet Nam-Egypt, Zambia-Egypt	1.64
Argentina-New Zealand, Argentina-Romania, Benin-Germany, Croatia-US, Czech Republic-India, Egypt-Albania, Egypt-Hungary, Egypt-Latvia, Egypt-Netherlands, Egypt-Nigeria, Egypt-Singapore, Egypt-Sri Lanka, Finland-Argentina, Germany-Bangladesh, Germany-Israel, Germany-Mali, Germany-Niger, Germany-Portugal, Germany-Togo, India-Brunei Darussalam, India-Jordan, Iran-Germany, Republic of Korea-Germany, Lesotho-Germany, Liberia-Germany, Malaysia-India, Morocco-India, Papua New Guinea-Germany, Senegal-India, Sri Lanka-US, Tunisia-Germany, Uganda-Germany, UK-Egypt, US-Azerbaijan, US-Bangladesh, US-Cameroon, US-Democratic Republic of the Congo, US-Czech, US-Ecuador, US-Estonia, US-Georgia, US-Grenada, US-Honduras, US-Jamaica, US-Kyrgyz Republic, US-Latvia, US-Lithuania, US-Moldova, US-Morocco, US-Mozambique, US-Trinidad and Tobago, US-Tunisia, US-Turkey, US-Ukraine, US-Uruguay, US-Uzbekistan, Zambia-Germany	1.73
Argentina-Croatia, Austria-India, Bangladesh-India, Central African Republic-Germany, Chile-Germany, PRC-Argentina, PRC-Egypt, Democratic Republic of the Congo-Germany, Dominica-Germany, Egypt-Armenia, Egypt-Czech Republic, Egypt-Italy, Egypt-Portugal, Egypt-Serbia, Egypt-Slovakia, France-India, Germany-Burundi, Germany-Chad, Germany-Cote D'Ivoire, Germany-Mauritania, Germany-Saint Lucia, Germany-Sierra Leone, Germany-Somalia, Germany-Trinidad and Tobago, Germany–Russian Federation, Germany-Yemen, Greece-India, Haiti-Germany, India-Armenia, India-Australia, India-Bahrain, India-Belarus, India-Belgium, India-Bosnia and Herzegovina, India-PRC, India-Croatia, India-Egypt, India-Finland, India-Hungary, India-Israel, India-Kazakhstan, India-Latvia, India-Mexico, India-Mongolia, India-Mozambique, India-Oman, India-Qatar, India-Russian Federation, India-Saudi Arabia, India-Spain, India-Sweden, India-Switzerland, India-Syrian Arab Republic, India-Taipei,China, India-Thailand, India-Trinidad and Tobago, India-Viet Nam, India-Yemen, Indonesia-Germany, Indonesia-India, Iran-Germany, Republic of Korea-Argentina, Republic of Korea-Egypt, Kuwait-India, Lao PDR-India, Libya-India, Macedonia-India, Malta-Germany, Mauritius-Germany, Mexico-Germany, Myanmar-India, Philippines-India, Poland-Germany, Poland-India, Russian Federation-Egypt, Saint Vincent and the Grenadines-Germany, Serbia-India, Slovakia-India, Sri Lanka-India, Sudan-Germany, Sudan-India, Swaziland-Germany, Tanzania-Germany, Thailand-Egypt, Turkey-Germany, Turkey-India, Turkmenistan-India, Ukraine-India, US-Albania, US -Bolivia, US-Senegal, US-Slovakia, Uzbekistan-India, Viet Nam-Germany, Zimbabwe-Germany	1.82

continued on the next page

Table 4 Continued

Algeria-Germany, Angola-Germany, Armenia-Germany, Azerbaijan-Germany, Bahrain-Germany, Barbados-Germany, Bolivia-Germany, Botswana-Germany, Burkina Faso-Germany, Cambodia-Germany, PRC-Germany, Costa Rica-Germany, Cuba-Germany, Cyprus-India, Czechoslovakia/Czech Republic-Germany, Czechoslovakia /Slovakia-Germany, Ecuador-Germany, Egypt-Denmark, Estonia-Germany, Ethiopia-Germany, Gabon-Germany, Germany-Afghanistan, Germany-Albania, Germany-Antigua and Barbuda, Germany-Argentina, Germany-Belarus, Germany-Bosnia and Herzegovina, Germany-Brazil, Germany-Brunei Darussalam, Germany-Cape Verde, Germany-Croatia, Germany-Egypt, Germany-El Salvador, Germany-Georgia, Germany-Guinea, Germany-Honduras, Germany-Hong Kong, China, Germany-India, Germany-Jordan, Germany-Kazakhstan, Germany-Latvia, Germany-Lebanon, Germany-Lithuania, Germany-Madagascar, Germany-Mongolia, Germany-Nepal, Germany-Philippines, Germany-Qatar, Germany-Romania, Germany-Tajikistan, Germany-Timor-Leste, Germany-Turkmenistan, Germany-Uzbekistan, Ghana-Germany, Greece-Egypt, Guatemala-Germany, Guyana-Germany, Hungary-Germany, India-Argentina, India-Bulgaria, India-Denmark, India-Kyrgyz Republic, India-Romania, India-Republic of Korea, India-Tajikistan, India-UK, Indonesia-Germany, Italy-India, Jamaica-Germany, Kenya-Germany, Kuwait-Germany, Kyrgyz Republic-Germany, Lao PDR-Germany, Libya-Germany, Macedonia, FYR-Germany, Mauritius-India, Moldova-Germany, Morocco-Germany, Mozambique-Germany, Namibia-Germany, Netherlands-India, Nicaragua-Germany, Nigeria-Germany, Oman-Germany, Panama-Germany, Paraguay-Germany, Peru-Germany, Portugal-India, Saudi Arabia-Germany, Slovenia-Germany, South Africa-Germany, Sri Lanka-Germany, Thailand-Germany, Ukraine-Germany, United Arab Emirates-Germany, Uruguay-Germany, US-Argentina, US-Democratic Republic of the Congo, Venezuela-Germany, Yemen-Germany, Yugoslavia/Serbia-Germany	1.91

FYR = former Yugoslav Republic, IIA = international investment agreement, PRC = People's Republic of China, UK = United Kingdom, US = United States.
Source: ADB International Investment Agreements Tool Kit.

The ADB IIA Tool Kit quality indicator can be summarized as a powerful tool to promptly evaluate an IIA strength. In this sense, it might be a suitable indicator to assess a great number of treaties to identify patterns over time, regions, or countries:

- First, Table 4 reveals that developed–developing, developing–developing, and developed economy pairs all appear across different levels of the ADB IIA Tool Kit quality indicator. This is equally true for the lowest and the highest levels of the indicator.

- Second, for many questions, it makes more sense to classify countries by the quality of their IIAs rather than just by the number of IIAs: Do economy pairs with more IIAs achieve higher FDI inflows or economy pairs with higher quality IIAs? Does higher quality of IIAs imply less risk for governments in pursuing policy changes? All these questions are derived from the Tool Kit data and offer potential for further research.

4.2.2   Indicator of Heterogeneity of IIAs

The indicator number itself expresses the relation of the standard deviation (a measure for the dispersion of the data) to their mean. It shows the extent of variability in relation to the mean of the population. If the indicator of variation is lower than 0.5, the mean value is a good representation for all data (Table 5). What does the indicator of variation say in comparison to other countries? Whereas the sum for each country tells us how investor-friendly the IIAs provisions are, the indicator of variation tells us how heterogeneous they are. The key advantage of the indicator of variation is that it is directly comparable between countries. If we have an indicator of variation for country A, say 30%, and for country B, say 60%, we can say that the heterogeneity of country B is twice as large as that for country A.

Heterogeneity of IIAs has many sources: level of development of a country (low, transition, high), the nature of the partner country, the timing of treaty conclusion, and so on. To illustrate this indicator, we have selected large countries, which have either a large number of BITs (like the PRC) or a small number of BITs (like Poland) and a long history of BIT-making, so that homogeneity can be excluded.

Table 5: ADB IIA Tool Kit Heterogeneity: Poland, People's Republic of China, Egypt, India, and United States

Economy Pairs	Indicator of Heterogeneity of IIAs (Coefficient of variance = S.D./Mean)
Austria-India, Egypt-Denmark, Germany-India, Greece-Egypt, India-Belgium, India-Denmark, India-Qatar, India-Spain, India-Switzerland, India-Tajikistan, India-UK, Kuwait-India, Mauritius-India, Netherlands-India, Turkmenistan-India	0.08
PRC-Egypt, Cyprus-India, Czech Republic-India, Egypt-Armenia, Egypt-Czech Republic, Egypt-Italy, Egypt-Portugal, Egypt-Serbia, Egypt-Slovakia, France-India, Greece-India, India-Argentina, India-Armenia, India-Australia, India-Bahrain, India-Belarus, India-Bosnia and Herzegovina, India-Brunei Darussalam, India-Bulgaria, India-PRC, India-Croatia, India-Egypt, India-Finland, India-Hungary, India-Israel, India-Jordan, India-Kazakhstan, India-Kyrgyz Republic, India-Latvia, India-Mongolia, India-Mozambique, India-Oman, India-Romania, India-Saudi Arabia, India-Sweden, India-Taipei,China, India-Thailand, India-Trinidad and Tobago, India-Viet Nam, India-Yemen, Indonesia-India, Italy-India, Republic of Korea-Egypt, Lao PDR-India, Libya-India, Macedonia-India, Malaysia-India, Morocco-India, Myanmar-India, Philippines-India, Poland-India, Portugal-India, Russian Federation-Egypt, Senegal-India, Serbia-India, Sri Lanka-India, Sudan-India, Thailand-Egypt, Ukraine-India, Uzbekistan-India	0.15
Belgium-PRC, Tunisia-PRC, US-Argentina, US-Democratic Republic of the Congo	0.16
Bangladesh-India, Egypt-Albania, Egypt-Hungary, Egypt-Latvia, Egypt-Netherlands, Egypt-Nigeria, Egypt-Singapore, Egypt-Sri Lanka, Iceland-India, India-Russian Federation, India-Republic of Korea, India-Syrian Arab Republic, Slovakia-India, Turkey-India, UK-Egypt	0.20
PRC-Democratic People's Republic of Korea, PRC-Netherlands, PRC-Sweden, US-Albania, US-Bolivia, US-Senegal, US-Slovakia	0.22
Chile-Egypt, Egypt-Australia, Egypt-Belarus, Egypt-Botswana, Egypt-Georgia, Egypt-Kazakhstan, Egypt-Pakistan, Egypt-Romania, Egypt-Turkmenistan, Egypt-Uganda, Egypt-Ukraine, Ghana-Egypt, India-Mexico, Indonesia-Egypt, Japan-Egypt, Malaysia-Egypt, US-Egypt, Viet Nam-Egypt, Zambia-Egypt	0.23
Egypt–Belgium–Luxembourg, Egypt-Bulgaria, Egypt-Canada, Egypt-Cyprus, Egypt-Macedonia, FYR, Egypt-Poland, Egypt-Sweden, Egypt-Turkey, Finland-Egypt, Jordan-Egypt	0.25

continued on the next page

Table 5 Continued

PRC-Albania, PRC-Benin, PRC-Denmark, PRC-Republic of Korea, PRC-Lebanon, PRC-Switzerland, Croatia-US, Czech Republic-PRC, Sri Lanka-US, US-Azerbaijan, US-Bahrain, US-Bangladesh, US-Cameroon, US-Democratic Republic of the Congo, US-Czech, US-Ecuador, US-Estonia, US-Georgia, US-Grenada, US-Honduras, US-Jamaica, US-Kyrgyz Republic, US-Latvia, US-Lithuania, US-Moldova, US-Morocco, US-Mozambique, US-Trinidad and Tobago, US-Tunisia, US-Turkey, US-Ukraine, US-Uruguay, US-Uzbekistan	0.27
Cambodia-PRC, Chile-PRC, PRC-Bolivia, PRC-Cote D'Ivoire, PRC-Germany, PRC-Guyana, PRC-Iran, PRC-Jamaica, PRC-Latvia, PRC-Mexico, PRC-Peru, PRC-Uganda, Croatia-PRC, El Salvador-US, Jordan-PRC, Jordan-US, Kuwait-PRC, Myanmar-PRC, New Zealand-PRC, Romania-US, Rwanda-US, US-Armenia, US-Bulgaria, US-Haiti, US-Kazakhstan, US-Mongolia, US-Nicaragua, US-Panama, US-Poland, US-Russian Federation, Viet Nam-PRC	0.31
Belize-PRC, Brunei Darussalam-PRC, Cameroon-PRC, PRC-Cuba, PRC-Estonia, PRC-Ethiopia, PRC-Georgia, PRC-Ghana, PRC-Greece, PRC-Iceland, PRC-Japan, PRC-Lithuania, PRC-Norway, PRC-Pakistan, PRC-Poland, PRC-Qatar, PRC-Singapore, PRC-Uruguay, Hungary-PRC, Lao PDR-PRC, Madagascar-PRC, Morocco-PRC, Portugal-PRC, Romania-PRC, Slovenia-PRC, Spain-PRC, Swaziland-PRC, Thailand-PRC, UK-PRC	0.34
Bulgaria-PRC, PRC-Argentina, PRC-Bahrain, PRC-Colombia, PRC-Costa Rica, PRC-Djibouti, PRC-Ecuador, PRC-Egypt, PRC-Slovakia, France-PRC, Italy-PRC, Philippines-PRC, Sri Lanka-PRC	0.36
Bosnia and Herzegovina-PRC, PRC-Australia, PRC-Botswana, PRC-Turkey, Indonesia-PRC, Mongolia-PRC, Trinidad and Tobago-PRC	0.37

FYR = former Yugoslav Republic, IIA = international investment agreement, Lao PDR = Lao People's Democratic Republic, PRC = People's Republic of China, S.D. = standard deviation, UK = United Kingdom, US = United States.
Source: ADB International Investment Agreements Tool Kit.

The indicator of variation that is extracted in Table 5 is probably the most puzzling ADB IIA Tool Kit indicator for most lawyers but it is also probably, by its very nature, one of the most interesting:

- First, the coefficient of variation for all countries is lower than 0.5 and hence the mean value of the ADB IIA Tool Kit quality indicator is a good representation for all BITs of a country.

- Second, however, the difference between the lowest (where in the majority of cases India is partner) and the highest indicator value (for economy pairs, where exclusively the PRC is partner) is strikingly large. This reflects obviously different patterns of two important BRICS economies, although both are also represented in all other categories. This may reflect the fast-evolving approach of treaty-making by the PRC, whereas India's approach has been more conservative. The United States is represented in the middle, showing a strong homogeneity (partly due to the existence and refinement of a US model BIT).

- These preliminary observations raise more fundamental issues. Is heterogeneity—with the exception of time—important for large countries with strong negotiating power or is it just the result of different partner countries? Does heterogeneity of IIAs lead to heterogeneity of FDI (in terms of investing industries, size, and so on)?

- From a theoretical perspective, one could question whether the large heterogeneity in IIAs may be a deterrent for regional (or multilateral) agreements. In a different way, one could also research how much heterogeneity contributes to legal complexity.

4.2.3   Modulation of Indicators' Force

The ADB IIA Tool Kit is not only an important tool to assess and analyze the impact of IIAs. It is also flexible enough to answer the needs of future research as it allows to modulate the importance allocated to various indicators. Indeed, when calculating the Quality Indicator (average), we rely on the score of 15 key provisions aggregated at cluster level. However, a concern may be that, for example, the same importance is given to the MFN clause and the duration of a treaty. Arguably, one could suggest that the MFN provision is far more important than a provision on the duration of the treaty. Indeed, the MFN clause, if extensively drafted and included in a treaty concluded by a country having a dense network of IIAs, can have considerable impact on investment decisions or arbitration results. In this regard, it is true that the likely effect of an MFN clause can be assumed to be greater than a provision on the duration. Hence, the weight given to these two values should be different.[58] The ADB IIA Tool Kit and the indicators developed do not ignore this reality. It is possible for any researcher to adjust the strength given to each score or agreement-level indicator. Three applications are now described which could be of interest for negotiators, drafting new treaties or considering adjustment of existing ones, when dealing with the precise wording of the provisions based on existing treaties.

- First, if one is comparing the relevance of certain provisions and, for example, takes the view that the MFN clause is a key feature of the People's Republic of China's investment treaties (because it allows foreign investors to take benefit of any greater advantage that the PRC would grant to any other foreigners), one can combine the number of the weak IIAs with the numbers of the strong IIAs. That means multiplying the number of the weak IIAs with the percentage of strong IIAs of that country. For example, if the weak IIA gets the indicator number 1, and 99% of the IIAs of that country have extensive MFN, we end up with a figure of 99. But if only 9% of the IIAs of that country have extensive MFN, we end up with 9. This saves research from using weights that are totally arbitrary.

- Second, this type of analysis will have its merits when variations *within certain provisions* are introduced: consider, for example, the provision on indirect expropriation. In some treaties, the definition of what constitutes indirect expropriation will be formulated in a more rigorous way than in others. Grouping the treaties by similarity of definitions of indirect expropriation would enrich any analysis beyond just including the information whether indirect expropriation is included in a treaty or not. It may well be that indirect expropriation will be used more often by claimants when certain criteria are listed in a treaty. Such indirect expropriation clauses in treaties could be given more weight. The weight for this grouping could be built on whether a government has been challenged on this provision before an arbitration court in the past.

- Third, apart from the single provisions, it may be of interest to consider whether groups of provisions, when included together in treaties, are more powerful in attracting FDI than when included as single provisions. For example, for highly profitable firms in skill-intensive industries, it will not only be vital whether indirect expropriation is included, but whether free flow of capital is included as well. For environmentally intensive production, it may be crucial whether more than one provision is included in a treaty which may be used to challenge changes in environmental regulation.

---

[58]   A similar concern can be raised in regard of the "breadth quality indicator" and the "guard quality indicator." Perhaps the latter, representing the combination of fair and equitable treatment and expropriation clause, is more important than the "breadth quality indicator."

The modulation of the ADB IIA Tool Kit indicators' force provides great flexibility and gives capacity to lawyers and other users to fine-tune the economic analysis. Over time, and depending on the case law, some provisions may take on more important roles than others. For instance, the FET provision was largely ignored until 2000–2009, possibly implying that no investor would take it into account at the time of the investment. However, after many disputes the FET has gained prominence in recent years. Some would argue that FET now has a greater role than do the expropriation clauses. The ADB IIA Tool Kit allows researchers to account for these and other changes in future. However, because the weighting remains highly subjective, other methods (such as principal components analysis) may provide more objective weights for analysis.

5. Conclusions

The IIAs provide a legal framework for international investment, and their proliferation during the last 50 years is the most striking phenomenon in the development of international investment law. With the number of bilateral investment treaties and preferential trade agreements that include an investment chapter continuing to expand, different standards and disciplines are beginning to be exerted over foreign investments. This gives substance to the complex universe of IIAs. The global regime for foreign investment is expanding amid greater diversity of agreements, rules, and principles, which the ADB IIA Tool Kit will help to investigate.

All stakeholders in this regime are developing new rules without being certain of their impacts and long-term effects. These stakeholders are: governments (including supranational entities such as the European Union), who are interested in the effect of IIAs on foreign direct investment (FDI); multinational enterprises, that want to know if the protection effect of IIAs is sufficient; lawyers, who examine whether the additional layer of bilateral agreements affects the scope and efficiency of laws governing international investment; and economists, who query whether efficiency can be raised by the current system of bilateralism through IIAs. The *common aspect* of all these questions relates to the contents and substance of agreements. The ADB IIA Tool Kit allows governments to assess questions about how the various types of IIAs affect FDI differently. It allows multinational enterprises to compare directly IIAs across a large number of countries where they have affiliates, and it allows lawyers to progress from the study of a single particular IIA toward a more universal and applied view of this part of international investment law. Lastly, the Tool Kit helps economists to develop a view on which provisions of IIAs are most similar and so could be extended to regional and multilateral agreements at the least cost.

The economic empirical literature is just starting to explore to what extent *treaty content* matters. As has been explained in this manual, treaty contents are reflected in great detail by the ADB IIA Tool Kit indicators. It is our hope that this Tool Kit will help to generate new research and questions to further improve the understanding of the international regime on foreign investment. The ADB IIA Tool Kit should provide stakeholders and users with a flexible and innovative tool for this purpose.

Bibliography

1. References

Asian Development Bank. 2021. *Asian Economic Integration Report 2021: Making Digital Platforms Work for Asia and the Pacific.* Manila.

Bath, V. and L. Nottage. 2011. Introduction. In V. Bath and L. Nottage, eds. *Investment Law and Dispute Resolution Law and Practice in Asia.* London: Routledge.

_____. 2013. The ASEAN Comprehensive Investment Agreement and 'ASEAN Plus'— The Australia–New Zealand Free Trade Area (AANZFTA) and the PRC–ASEAN Investment Agreement. *Sydney Law School Research Paper.* 13 (69). Sydney.

_____. 2019. Asian Investment and the Growth of Regional Investment Agreements. In C. Antons, ed. *Routledge Handbook of Asian Law.* London: Routledge.

Bellak, C. 2015. Economic Impact of Investment Agreements. *Department of Economics Working Paper.* No. 200. Vienna: Vienna University of Economics and Business.

Berger, A. and K. Sauvant, eds. 2021. *Investment Facilitation for Development: A Toolkit for Policymakers.* Geneva: International Trade Centre. https://www.intracen.org/uploadedFiles/intracenorg/Content/Publications/Investment%20Facilitation%20for%20Development_rev.Low-res.pdf

Bernasconi-Osterwalder, N. and D. Rosert. 2014. *Investment Treaty Arbitration: Opportunities to Reform Arbitral Rules and Processes.* Geneva: International Institute for Sustainable Development. http://www.iisd.org/publications/investment-treaty-arbitration-opportunities-reform-arbitral-rules-and-processes.

Bernasconi-Osterwalder N., S. Brewin, and N. Maina. 2020. Protecting Against Investor–State Claims Amidst COVID-19: A Call to Action for Governments. International Institute for Sustainable Investment (IISD) Commentary. April. https://www.iisd.org/system/files/publications/investor-state-claims-covid-19.pdf.

Bjorklund, A. 2010. The National Treatment Obligation. In K. Yannaca-Small, ed. *Arbitration Under International Investment Agreements: A Guide to the Key Issues.* Oxford: Oxford University Press.

Black's Law Dictionary. 2004. 8th Edition (Black's Law Dictionary (Standard Edition). Thomson West Publishing.

Chaisse, J. and C. Bellak. 2015. Navigating the Expanding Universe of International Treaties on Foreign Investment—Creation and Use of a Critical Index. *Journal of International Economic Law.* 18 (1). pp. 79–115.

Chaisse, J. 2015a. The Shifting Tectonics of International Investment Law—Structure and Dynamics of Rules and Arbitration on Foreign Investment in the Asia-Pacific Region. *The George Washington International Law Review.* 47 (3). pp. 563–638.

_____. 2015b. Admission Clause and Establishment. Lecture presentation for the Class of International Investment Law and Arbitration. University of Melbourne. 29 September.

Barnali C. 2008. Recapturing Public Power: Is Investment Arbitration's Engagement of the Public Interest Contributing to the Democratic Deficit? *Vanderbilt Journal of Transnational Law.* 41 (3). pp. 775-832.

Clifford Chance. 2015. The China Australia Free Trade Agreement – Investment Chapter. *Clifford Chance Briefing Notes.* https://www.cliffordchance.com/content/dam/cliffordchance/briefings/2015/07/the-china-australia-free-trade-agreement-investment-chapter.pdf.

Dolzer, R. and C. Schreuer. 2012. *Principles of International Investment Law.* Oxford: Oxford University Press.

Elkins, Z., A. Guzman, and B. Simmons. 2006. Competing for Capital: The Diffusion of Bilateral Investment Treaties, 1960–2000. *International Organization.* 60 (4). pp. 811–46.

Haftel, Y. and A. Thompson. 2013. Delayed Ratification: The Domestic Fate of Bilateral Investment Treaties. *International Organization.* 67 (2). pp. 355–87.

Jandhyala, S., W. Henisz, and E. Mansfield. 2011. Three Waves of BITs: The Global Diffusion of Foreign Investment Policy. *Journal of Conflict Resolution.* 55 (6). pp. 1047–73.

Kalicki, J. and S. Medeiros. 2007. Fair, Equitable and Ambiguous: What is Fair and Equitable Treatment in International Investment Law? *ICSID Review—Foreign Investment Law Journal.* 22 (1). pp. 24–54.

Kaushal, A. 2009. Revisiting History: How the Past Matters for the Present Backlash against the Foreign Investment Regime. *Harvard International Law Journal.* 50 (2). pp. 491–534.

Knorich, J. and A. Berger. 2014. Friends or Foes? Interactions between Indonesia's International Investment Agreement and National Investment Law. *Studies.* 82 (82). Bonn: German Development Institute.

Lowenfeld, A. 2008. *International Economic Law.* Oxford: Oxford University Press.

Naon, H. 1996. Sovereignty and Regionalism. *Law and Policy in International Business.* 27 (4). pp. 1077–78.

Newcombie, A. and L. Paradell. 2009. *Law and Practice of Investment Treaties: Standards of Treatment.* Alphen aan den Rijn: Wolters Kluwer Law & Business.

Nottage, L. 2016. The TPP Investment Chapter and Investor–State Arbitration in Asia and Oceania: Assessing Prospects for Ratification. *Melbourne Journal of International Law.* 17 (2). pp. 1–36.

Organisation for Economic Co-operation and Development (OECD). 2019. *FDI Qualities Indicators: Measuring the Sustainable Development Impacts of Investment.* Paris. www.oecd.org/fr/investissement/fdi-qualities-indicators.htm.

Poulsen, L. 2010. Bilateral Investment Treaties and Preferential Trade Agreements: Is a BIT Really Better Than a Lot?. *Investment Treaty News Quarterly.* 1 (1). p. 16. September.

Ranjan, P. and P. Anand. 2020. COVID-19, India, and Investor-State Dispute Settlement (ISDS): Will India Be Able to Defend Its Public Health Measures?. *Asia Pacific Law Review.* 28 (1). pp. 225–47. DOI: 10.1080/10192557.2020.1812255.

Reinisch, A. 2013. The Scope of Investor-State Dispute Settlement in International Investment Agreements. *Asia Pacific Law Review.* 21 (1). pp. 3-26. DOI: 10.1080/10192557.2013.11788264.

Sacerdoti, G. 2000. The Admission and Treatment of Foreign Investment under Recent Bilateral and Regional Treaties. *Journal of World Investment and Trade.* 1 (1). pp. 105–26.

Salacuse, J. 2010. The Emerging Global Regime for Investment. *Harvard International Law Journal.* 51 (2). pp. 427–31.

Salacuse, J. 2013. *The Three Laws of International Investment: National, Contractual, and International Frameworks for Foreign Capital.* Oxford: Oxford University Press.

Saurav, A., P. Kusek, R. Kuo, and B. Viney. 2020. The Impact of COVID-19 on Foreign Investors: Evidence from the Second Round of a Global Pulse Survey. *World Bank Blogs.* 6 October. https://blogs.worldbank.org/psd/impact-covid-19-foreign-investors-evidence-second-round-global-pulse-survey.

Subedi, S. 2012. *International Investment Law: Reconciling Policy and Principle.* London: Hart Publishing.

United Nations Conference on Trade and Development (UNCTAD). 1999. *National Treatment, UNCTAD Series on Issues in International Investment Agreements.* New York and Geneva: United Nations.

_____. 2007. *Bilateral Investment Treaties 1995–2006: Trends in Investment Rulemaking.* New York and Geneva: United Nations.

_____. 2014. *World Investment Report 2014.* New York and Geneva: United Nations.

_____. 2016. UNCTAD Facilitates G20 Consensus on Guiding Principles for Global Investment Policymaking. *UNCTAD News Report.* 11 July. http://investmentpolicyhub.unctad.org/News/Hub/Home/508.

_____. 2020. International Investment Agreements Navigator. https://investmentpolicy.unctad.org/ international-investment-agreements.

_____. 2020. International Investment Agreements Reform Accelerator. https://unctad.org/system/files/official-document/diaepcbinf2020d8_en.pdf.

Vandevelde, K. 2005. A Brief History of International Investment Agreements. *U.C. Davis Journal of International Law & Policy.* 12 (1). pp. 157–94.

Vandevelde, K. 2010. *Bilateral Investment Treaties: History, Policy, and Interpretation.* Oxford: Oxford University Press.

Wang, G. 2010. International Investment Law: An Appraisal from the Perspective of the New Haven School of International Law. *Asia Pacific Law Review.* 18 (1). pp. 19–44. DOI: 10.1080/ 10192557.2010.11788222.

Weeramantry, J. 2012. Investor-State Dispute Settlement Provisions in China's Investment Treaties. *ICSID Review—Foreign Investment Law Journal.* 27 (1). pp. 192–206.

Wei, Y. 2018. Challenges, Issues in China-EU Investment Agreement and the Implication on China's Domestic Reform. *Asia Pacific Law Review.* 26 (2). pp. 170-202. DOI: 10.1080/10192557.2019.1576347.

Williams, D. 2001. Policy Perspectives on the Use of Capital Controls in Emerging Nations: Lessons From the Asian Financial Crisis and a Look at the International Legal Regime. *Fordham Law Review.* 70 (2). pp. 561–621.

Yannaca-Small, K. 2010. Fair and Equitable Treatment Standard. In K. Yannaca-Small, ed. *Arbitration Under International Investment Agreements: A Guide to the Key Issues.* Oxford: Oxford University Press.

2. Treaties Cited

Agreement between The Government of Denmark and The Government of The Republic of Indonesia Concerning The Encouragement and The Reciprocal Protection of Investments, signed 30 January 1968, [1970] UNTS 224 (entered into force 2 July 1968).

Agreement between the Government of the United Kingdom of Great Britain and Northern Ireland and the Government of the Republic of Indonesia for the Promotion and Protection of Investments, signed 27 April 1976, (1977) Treaty Series 62 (entered into force 24 March 1977).

Agreement between the Government of Australia and the Government of the Republic Indonesia concerning the Promotion and Protection of Investment, signed 17 November 1992, [1993] ATS 19 (entered into force 29 July 1993).

Agreement between the Government of the Republic Indonesia and the Government of the Republic of Uzbekistan concerning the Promotion and Protection of Investment, signed 27 August 1996 (entered into force 27 April 1997).

Agreement between the Government of the Republic of Indonesia and the Government of the Kingdom of Morocco for the Promotion and Protection of Investments, signed 14 March 1997 (entered into force 21 March 2002).

Agreement between the Government of the Republic of Singapore and the Government of the Republic of Indonesia on the Promotion and Protection of Investment, signed 16 February 2005 (entered into force 21 June 2006).

Agreement between the Government of the Republic of Finland and the Government of the Republic of Indonesia for the Promotion and Protection of Investments, signed 12 September 2006 (entered into force 2 August 2008).

ASEAN Comprehensive Investment Agreement, signed 26 February 2009 (entered into force 29 March 2012).

Treaty between the United States of America and the Arab Republic of Egypt Concerning the Reciprocal Encouragement and Protection of Investment, signed 11 March 1986 (entered into force 27 June 1992).

The North American Free Trade Agreement, signed 17 December 1992, 32 ILM 289 and 605 (entered into force 1 January 1994) Chapter 11 ('NAFTA').

The US BIT Model 2004.

The United States-Uruguay BIT 2005.

3. Other Resources

Amianti, G. 2005. Government Revises Investment Treaties. *The Jakarta Post*. News release. 12 May. http://www.thejakartapost.com/news/2015/05/12/govt-revises-investment-treaties.html.

Darmawan, S. and Sakurayuki. 2014. Indonesia Revises Its Negative Investment List for New Foreign Direct Investment. *Herbert Smith Freehills*. May.

Indonesia Investment Coordinating Board. 2015. *Domestic and Foreign Direct Investment Realization Steadily Increased, Beyond the Annual Target of 2014*. Press Release, 28 January. http://www.indonesia-investments.com/upload/documents/BKPM-Press-Release-Investment-Realization-2014-Indonesia-Investments.pdf.

Maryati and A. Hasanah. 2015. Unprofitable Bilateral Investment Treaties Need to be Revised. *Voice of Indonesia*. 14 May. http://en.voi.co.id/voi-editorial/8974-unprofitable-bilateral-investment-treaties-need-to-be-revised.

Oegroseno, A. 2014. Revamping Bilateral Treaties. *The Jakarta Post*. News release. 7 July. http://www.thejakartapost.com/news/2014/07/07/revamping-bilateral-treaties.html.

UNCTAD. *Indonesia: Bilateral Investment Treaties*. New York and Geneva: United Nations. http://investmentpolicyhub.unctad.org/IIA/CountryBits/97#iiaInnerMenu.

Annex I. Data Organization

A. ADB International Investment Agreement (IIA) Tool Kit (dataset)

A dataset is a collection of numerical values with associated textual information. All values share a common set of dimensions. The present dataset features more than 1,200 BITs and more than 200 FTAs; each of these treaties has its 14 main provisions classified. The dataset provides information on more than 21,000 provisions.

B. Other available information

The ADB IIA Tool Kit also features five technical features which are not coded but can be helpful to analyze treaties.

1. Date of Signature

The Date of Signature is the date when representatives of both countries sign the text to become a party to a treaty. A State must express its consent to be bound by the treaty. Such consent can be expressed in a variety of ways, including through signature of the treaty by a proper representative of the State.

2. Date Entry into Force

The date on which both the parties fulfill the domestic requirement for such entry into force, which in most cases means ratification by the national parliaments. The treaty becomes effective after notification stating that requirements are fulfilled by both parties to each other.

3. Termination period

It is the period for which a treaty shall remain in force, for instance 10 or 15 years, and after which treaty stands automatically terminated.

4. Notice-time for treaty cancellation

In most cases, a treaty may be terminated after it is entered into force if either of the parties gives a notice to the other party in writing stating their intention to terminate the treaty. The notice should be submitted to the other contracting party in advance, for example 6 months or 12 months.

5. New time period after normal treaty period

It usually specifies the time period for which an enforced treaty can be renewed, if both the parties agree.

Annex II.   Examples of IIA Tool Kit Indicators

1. Liberalization Quality Indicator, by Economy

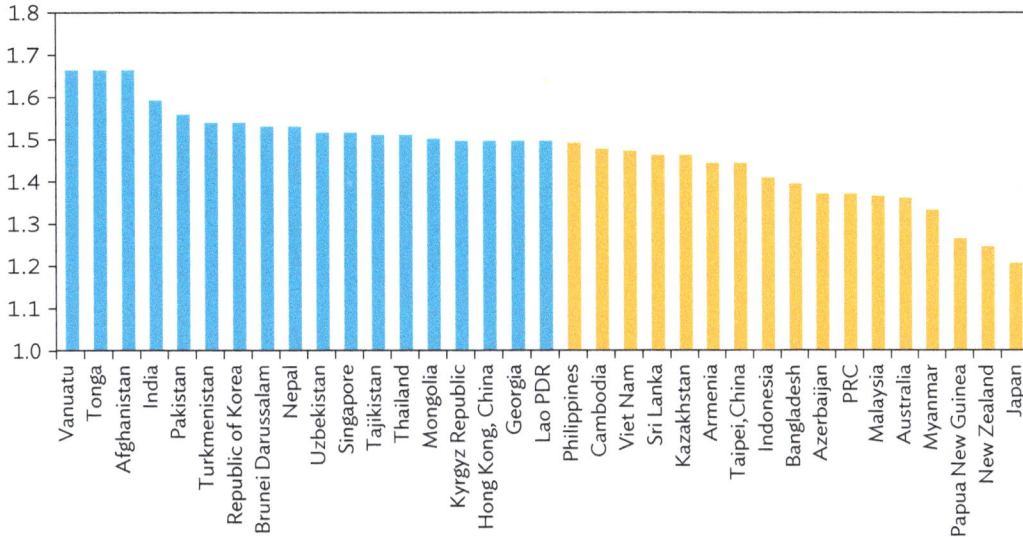

Lao PDR = Lao People's Democratic Republic, PRC = People's Republic of China.
Note: The Liberalization Quality Indicator measures the degree of openness of an economy to foreign investment, or, alternatively, the degree of control still maintained by a state over foreign investment.
Source: Authors' calculation, based on ADB database on International Investment Agreements (https://aric.adb.org/database/iias).

2. Anti-discrimination Quality Indicator, by Economy

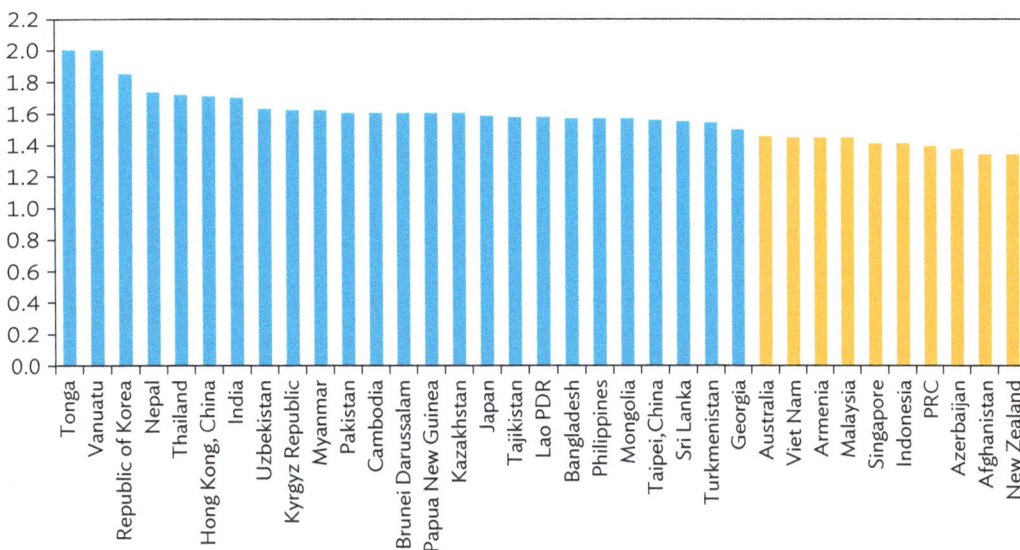

Lao PDR = Lao People's Democratic Republic, PRC = People's Republic of China.
Note: The Anti-discrimination Quality Indicator measures the degree to which International Investment Agreements (IIAs) ensure a certain degree of equality for foreigners (among themselves and/or vis-à-vis the nationals).
Source: Authors' calculation, based on ADB database on International Investment Agreements (https://aric.adb.org/database/iias).

3. Breadth Quality Indicator, by Economy

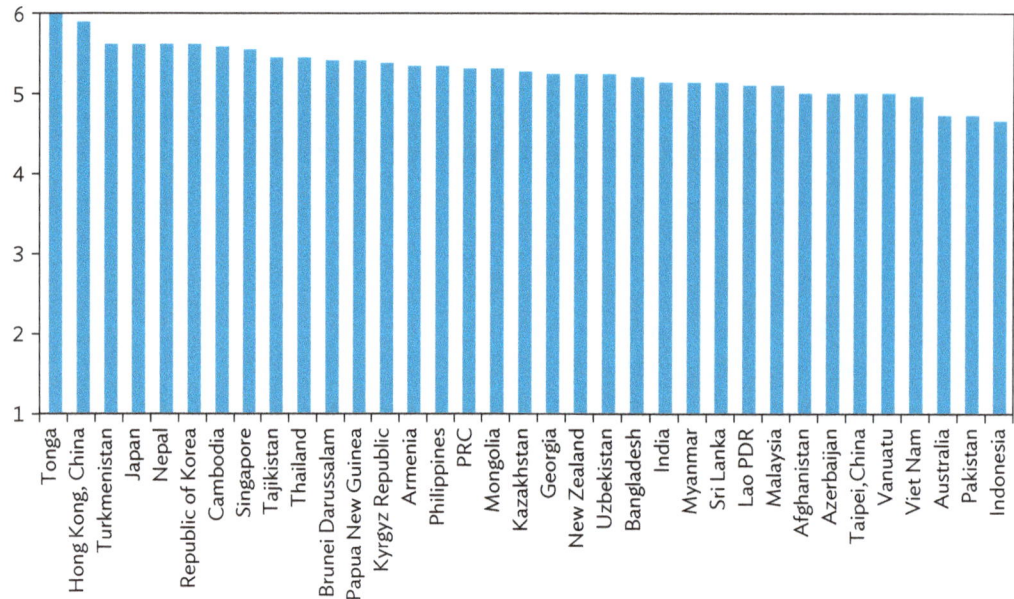

Lao PDR = Lao People's Democratic Republic, PRC = People's Republic of China.
Note: The Breadth Quality Indicator provides a measure of a country's potential scope of application in investment agreements.
Source: Authors' calculation, based on ADB database on International Investment Agreements (https://aric.adb.org/database/iias).

4. Regulatory Constraint Indicator, by Economy

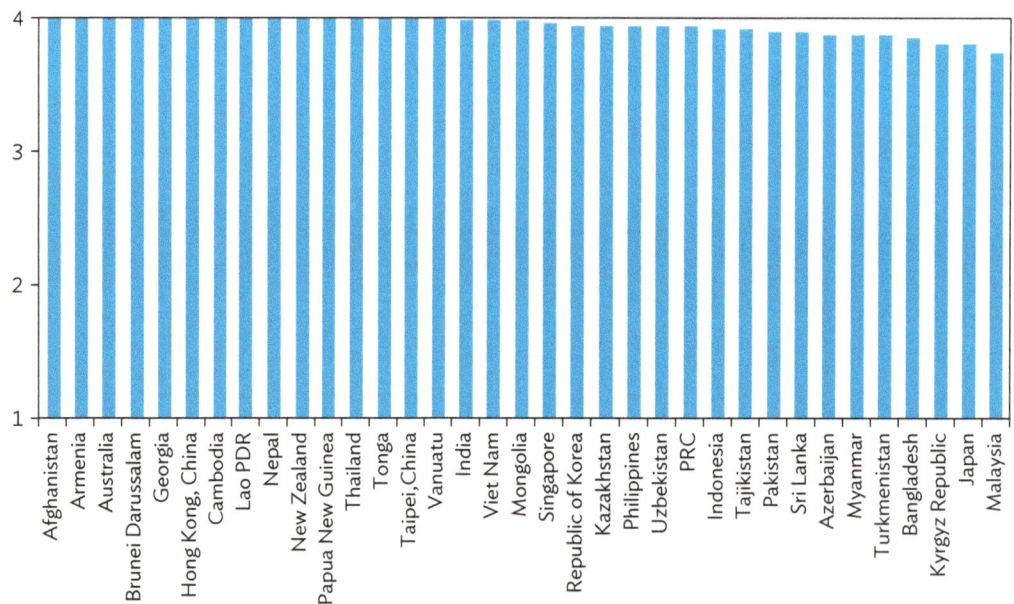

FET = fair and equitable treatment, IIA = international investment agreement, Lao PDR = Lao People's Democratic Republic, PRC = People's Republic of China.
Note: The Regulatory Constraint Quality Indicator provides a measure of the degree to which foreign investments are protected by IIAs. It does this by combining the score of expropriation and FET provisions.
Source: Authors' calculation, based on ADB database on International InvestmentAgreements (https://aric.adb.org/database/iias).

5. ISDS Quality Indicator, by Economy

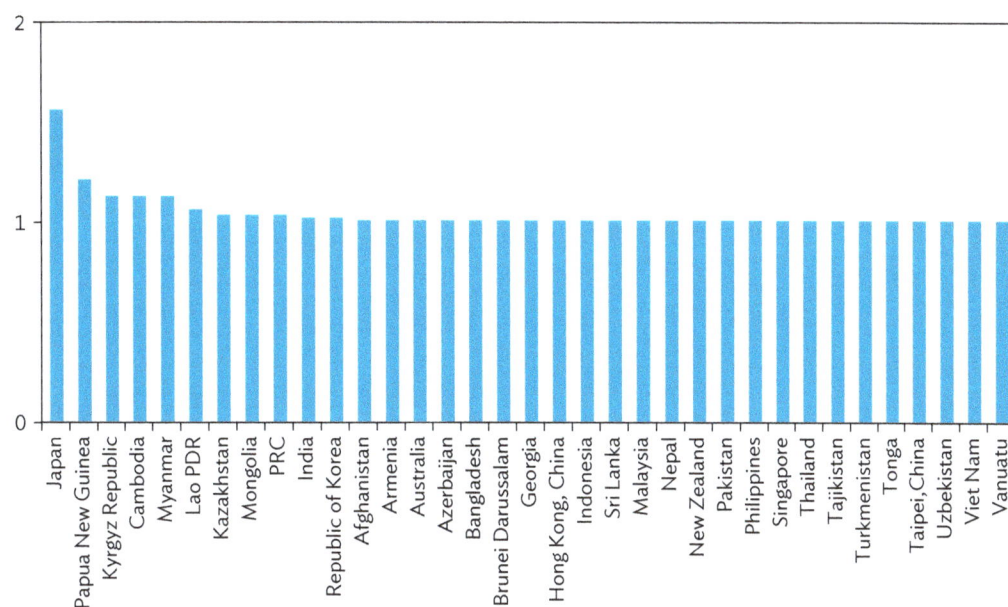

IIA = international investment agreement, ISDS = investor–state dispute settlement, Lao PDR = Lao People's Democratic Republic, PRC = People's Republic of China.

The ISDS Quality Indicator represents the average across ISDS provisions for all IIAs of a particular country. The higher the index, the greater is the access to Investor–State Arbitration facilitated and offered to foreign investment.

Source: Authors' calculation, based on ADB database on International Investment Agreements (https://aric.adb.org/database/iias).